I0161962

Bonduca by John Fletcher

John Fletcher was born in December, 1579 in Rye, Sussex. He was baptised on December 20th.

As can be imagined details of much of his life and career have not survived and, accordingly, only a very brief indication of his life and works can be given.

Young Fletcher appears at the very young age of eleven to have entered Corpus Christi College at Cambridge University in 1591. There are no records that he ever took a degree but there is some small evidence that he was being prepared for a career in the church.

However what is clear is that this was soon abandoned as he joined the stream of people who would leave University and decamp to the more bohemian life of commercial theatre in London.

The upbringing of the now teenage Fletcher and his seven siblings now passed to his paternal uncle, the poet and minor official Giles Fletcher. Giles, who had the patronage of the Earl of Essex may have been a liability rather than an advantage to the young Fletcher. With Essex involved in the failed rebellion against Elizabeth Giles was also tainted.

By 1606 John Fletcher appears to have equipped himself with the talents to become a playwright. Initially this appears to have been for the Children of the Queen's Revels, then performing at the Blackfriars Theatre.

Fletcher's early career was marked by one significant failure; The Faithful Shepherdess, his adaptation of Giovanni Battista Guarini's Il Pastor Fido, which was performed by the Blackfriars Children in 1608.

By 1609, however, he had found his stride. With his collaborator John Beaumont, he wrote Philaster, which became a hit for the King's Men and began a profitable association between Fletcher and that company. Philaster appears also to have begun a trend for tragicomedy.

By the middle of the 1610s, Fletcher's plays had achieved a popularity that rivalled Shakespeare's and cemented the pre-eminence of the King's Men in Jacobean London. After his frequent early collaborator John Beaumont's early death in 1616, Fletcher continued working, both singly and in collaboration, until his own death in 1625. By that time, he had produced, or had been credited with, close to fifty plays.

Index of Contents

BONDUCA

DRAMATIS PERSONAE
MEN
Caratach, General of the Britains, Cosin to Bonduca
Nenius, A great Soldier, a Britain Commander
Hengo, A brave boy, Nephew to Caratach
Swetonius, General to the Roman Army in Britain
Penyus, A brave Roman Commander, but stubborn to the General
Junius, A Roman Captain, in love with Bonduca's Daughter
Petillius, A merry Captain, but somewhat wanton
Demetrius, Decius, Two Roman Commanders
Regulus, Drusus, Macer, Curius, Four Roman Officers
Judas, A Corporal, a merry hungry knave
Herald
Druids
Soldiers
WOMEN
Bonduca, Queen of the Iceni, a brave Virago, by Prosutagus
Her two Daughters

THE SCENE: Britain

Enter **BONDUCA, DAUGHTERS, HENGO, NENNIUS, SOLDIERS.**

BONDUCA
The hardy Romans? O ye gods of Britain,
The rust of Arms, the blushing shame of soldiers;
Are these the men that conquer by inheritance!
The Fortune-makers? these the Julians.

[Enter **CARATACH.**

That with the Sun measure the end of Nature,
Making the World but one Rome and one Cæsar?
Shame, how they flee! Cæsars soft soul dwells in 'em;
Their Mothers got 'em sleeping, Pleasure nurst 'em,
Their Bodies sweat with sweet Oils, Loves allurements,
Not lustie Arms. Dare they send these to seek us,
These Roman Girls? Is Britain grown so wanton?
Twice we have beat 'em, Nennius scatter'd 'em,
And through their big-bon'd Germans, on whose Pikes
The honour of their actions sit in triumph,
Made Themes for Songs to shame 'em, and a Woman,
A Woman beat 'em, Nennius; a weak Woman,
A Woman beat these Romans.

CARATACH
So it seems.
A man would shame to talk so.

BONDUCA
Who's that?

CARATACH
I.

BONDUCA
Cosin, do you grieve at my fortunes?

CARATACH
No, Bonduca,
If I grieve, 'tis at the bearing of your fortunes;
You put too much wind to your sail: Discretion
And hardy valour are the twins of honour,
And nurs'd together, make a Conqueror:
Divided, but a talker. 'Tis a truth.

That Rome has fled before us twice, and routed;
A truth we ought to crown the gods for, Lady,
And not our tongues. A truth is none of ours,
Nor in our ends, more than the noble bearing:
For then it leaves to be a virtue, Lady;
And we that have been Victors, beat our selves,
When we insult upon our honors subject.

BONDUCA
My valiant Cosin, is it foul to say
What liberty and honor bid us do,
And what the gods allow us?

CARATACH
No, Bonduca,
So what we say exceed not what we do.
Ye call the Romans fearful, fleeing Romans,
And Roman Girls, the lees of tainted pleasures:
Does this become a doer? are they such?

BONDUCA
They are no more.

CARATACH
Where is your Conquest then?
Why are your Altars crown'd with wreaths of flowers,
The beasts with gilt horns waiting for the fire?
The holy Druides composing Songs
Of everlasting life to Victory?
Why are these triumphs, Lady? for a May-game?
For hunting a poor herd of wretched Romans?
Is it no more? shut up your Temples, Britains,
And let the Husbandman redeem his heifers;
Put out our holy fires; no Timbrel ring;
Let's home, and sleep; for such great overthrows;
A Candle burns too bright a sacrifice,
A Glow-worms tail too full of flame. O Nennius,
Thou hadst a noble Uncle knew a Roman,
And how to speak him, how to give him weight
In both his fortunes.

BONDUCA
By—I think
Ye doat upon these Romans, Caratach.

CARATACH
Witness these wounds, I do; they were fairly given,
I love an enemy, I was born a Soldier;

And he that in the head on's Troop defies me,
Bending my manly Body with his sword,
I make a Mistriss. Yellow-tressed Hymen
Ne'r ty'd a longing Virgin with more joy,
Than I am married to that man that wounds me:
And are not all these Romans? Ten struck Battels
I suck'd these honour'd scars from, and all Roman:
Ten years of bitter nights and heavy marches,
When many a frozen storm sung thorow my Curasse,
And made it doubtful whether that or I
Were the more stubborn metall, have I wrought thorow,
And all to try these Romans. Ten times a night
I have swom the Rivers, when the Stars of Rome
Shot at me as I floated, and the billows
Tumbled their watry ruines on my shoulders,
Charging my batter'd sides with troops of Agues;
And still to try these Romans, whom I found
(And if I lye, my wounds be henceforth backward,
And be you witness, gods, and all my dangers)
As ready, and as full of that I brought
(Which was not fear nor flight) as valiant,
As vigilant, as wise, to do and suffer,
Ever advanced as forward as the Britains,
Their sleeps as short, their hopes as high as ours.
I, and as subtil, Lady. 'Tis dishonour,
And follow'd, will be impudence, Bonduca,
And grow to no belief, to taint these Romans.
Have not I seen the Britains—

BONDUCA
What?

CARATACH
Disheartned,
Run, run, Bonduca, not the quick rack swifter;
The Virgin from the hated Ravisher
Not half so fearful; not a flight drawn home.
A round stone from a sling, a Lovers wish
E'r made that haste that they have. By—
I have seen these Britains, that you magnifie,
Run as they would have out-run time and roaring
Basely for mercy, roaring: the light shadows,
That in a thought scur o'r the fields of Corn,
Halted on crutches to 'em.

BONDUCA
O ye Powers,
What scandals do I suffer!

CARATACH

Yes, Bonduca,
I have seen thee run too, and thee, Nennius;
Yea, run apace, both; then when Penyus
The Roman Girl, cut thorow your armed Carts,
And drive 'em headlong on ye down the hill:
Then when he hunted ye like Britain-Foxes,
More by the scent than sight: then did I see
These valiant and approved men of Britain,
Like boading Owls, creep into tods of Ivie,
And hoot their fears to one another nightly.

NENNIUS

And what did you then, Caratach?

CARATACH

I fled too,
But not so fast; your Jewel had been lost then,
Young Hengo there; he trasht me, Nennius:
For when your fears out-run him, then stept I,
And in the head of all the Romans fury
Took him, and, with my tough Belt, to my back
I buckled him: behind him, my sure Shield;
And then I follow'd. If I say I fought
Five times in bringing off this bud of Britain,
I lye not, Nennius. Neither had ye heard
Me speak this, or ever seen the child more,
But that the Son of Virtue, Penyus
Seeing me steer thorow all these storms of danger,
My Helm still in my hand, my Sword my prow,
Turn'd to my foe my face, he cry'd out nobly,
Go Britain, bear thy Lions whelp off safely;
Thy manly sword has ransom'd thee: grow strong,
And let me meet thee once again in Arms;
Then if thou stand'st, thou art mine. I took his offer,
And here I am to honour him.

BONDUCA

O Cousin,
From what a flight of honour hast thou checkt me!
What wouldst thou make me, Caratach?

CARATACH

See, Lady,
The noble use of others in our losses:
Does this afflict ye? Had the Romans cry'd this,
And as we have done theirs, sung out these fortunes,

Rail'd on our base condition, hooted at us,
Made marks as far as the earth was ours, to shew us
Nothing but sea could stop our flights; despis'd us,
And held it equal, whether banqueting
Or beating of the Britains were more business,
It would have gall'd ye.

BONDUCA
Let me think we conquer'd.

CARATACH
Do; but so think, as we may be conquer'd:
And where we have found virtue, though in those
That came to make us slaves, let's cherish it.
There's not a blow we gave since Julius landed,
That was of strength and worth, but like records,
They file to after-ages. Our Registers,
The Romans, are for noble deeds of honour;
And shall we burn their mentions with upbraidings?

BONDUCA
No more, I see my self: thou hast made me, Cousin,
More than my fortunes durst, for they abus'd me,
And wound me up so high, I swell'd with glory:
Thy temperance has cur'd that Tympany,
And given me health again, nay, more discretion.
Shall we have peace? for now I love these Romans.

CARATACH
Thy love and hate are both unwise ones, Lady.

BONDUCA
Your reason?

NENNIUS
Is not peace the end of Arms?

CARATACH
Not where the cause implies a general conquest:
Had we a difference with some petty Isle,
Or with our neighbors (Lady) for our Land-marks,
The taking in of some rebellious Lord,
Or making a head against Commotions,
After a day of Blood, Peace might be argued:
But where we grapple for the ground we live on,
The Liberty we hold as dear as life,
The gods we worship, and next those, our Honors,
And with those swords that know no end of Battel:

Those men beside themselves allow no neighbor;
Those minds that where the day is, claim inheritance,
And where the Sun makes ripe the fruits, their harvest,
And where they march, but measure out more ground
To add to Rome, and here i'th' bowels on us;
It must not be; no, as they are our foes,
And those that must be so until we tire 'em,
Let's use the peace of Honor, that's fair dealing,
But in our ends, our swords. That hardy Romane
That hopes to graft himself into my stock,
Must first begin his kindred under-ground,
And be alli'd in ashes.

BONDUCA
Caratach,
As thou hast nobly spoken, shall be done;
And Hengo to thy charge I here deliver:
The Romans shall have worthy Wars.

CARATACH
They shall.
And, little Sir, when your young bones grow stiffer,
And when I see ye able in a morning
To beat a dozen boys, and then to breakfast,
I'll tye ye to a sword.

HENGO
And what then Uncle?

CARATACH
Then ye must kill, Sir, the next valiant Romane that
calls ye knave.

HENGO
And must I kill but one?

CARATACH
An hundred, boy, I hope.

HENGO
I hope five hundred.

CARATACH
That's a noble boy. Come, worthy Lady,
Let's to our several charges, and henceforth
Allow an enemy both weight and worth.

[Exeunt.

Enter **JUNIUS** and **PETILLIUS**, two Roman **CAPTAINS**.

PETILLIUS
What ail'st thou, man? dost thou want meat?

JUNIUS
No.

PETILLIUS
Clothes?

JUNIUS
Neither. For heavens love, leave me.

PETILLIUS
Drink?

JUNIUS
Ye tire me.

PETILLIUS
Come, 'tis drink; I know 'tis drink.

JUNIUS
Tis no drink.

PETILLIUS
I say 'tis drink: for what affliction
Can light so heavy on a Soldier,
To dry him up as thou art, but no drink?
Thou shalt have drink.

JUNIUS
Prethee Petillius—

PETILLIUS
And by mine honor, much drink, valiant drink:
Never tell me, thou shalt have drink. I see,
Like a true friend, into thy wants: 'tis drink;
And when I leave thee to a desolation,
Especially of that dry nature, hang me.

JUNIUS

Why do you do this to me?

PETILLIUS
For I see,
Although your modesty would fain conceal it,
Which sits as sweetly on a Soldier,
As an old side-saddle.

JUNIUS
What do you see?

PETILLIUS
I see as far as day, that thou want'st drink.
Did I not find thee gaping like an Oyster
For a new tide? thy very thoughts lie bare
Like a low ebb? thy Soul that rid in Sack,
Lies moor'd for want of liquor? Do but see
Into thy self; for by—I do:
For all thy body's chapt and crackt like timber
For want of moisture, what is't thou wantst there, Junius,
And if it be not drink?

JUNIUS
You have too much on't.

PETILLIUS
It may be a whore too; say it be; come, meecher,
Thou shalt have both, a pretty valiant fellow,
Die for a little lap and lechery?
No, it shall ne'r be said in our Countrey,
Thou dy'dst o'th' Chin-cough. Hear, thou noble Roman,
The Son of her that loves a Soldier,
Hear what I promised for thee; thus I said,
Lady, I take thy Son to my companion,
Lady, I love thy son, thy Son loves War,
The war loves danger, danger drink, drink discipline,
Which is society and lechery;
These two beget Commanders: fear not, Lady,
Thy Son shall lead.

JUNIUS
'Tis a strange thing, Petillius,
That so ridiculous and loose a mirth
Can master your affections.

PETILLIUS
Any mirth,
And any way, of any subject, Junius,

Is better than unmanly mustiness:
What harm's in drink, in a good wholsome wench?
I do beseech ye, Sir, what error? yet
It cannot out of my head handsomely,
But thou wouldst fain be drunk: come, no more fooling,
The General has new wine, new come over.

JUNIUS
He must have new acquaintance for it too,
For I will none, I thank ye.

PETILLIUS
None I thank ye?
A short and touchie answer. None I thank ye:
Ye do not scorn it, do ye?

JUNIUS
Gods defend, Sir;
I owe him still more honor.

PETILLIUS
None, I thank ye:
No company, no drink, no wench, I thank ye.
Ye shall be worse intreated, Sir.

JUNIUS
Petillius,
As thou art honest, leave me.

PETILLIUS
None, I thank ye;
A modest and a decent resolution,
And well put on. Yes, I will leave ye, Junius,
And leave ye to the boys, that very shortly
Shall all salute ye, by your new sirname
Of Junius None I thank ye. I would starve now,
Hang, drown, despair, deserve the forks, lie open
To all the dangerous passes of a wench,
Bound to believe her tears, and wed her aches,
E'r I would own thy follies. I have found ye,
Your lays, and out-leaps Junius, haunts, and lodges:
I have view'd ye, and I have found ye by my skill
To be a fool o'th' first head, Junius,
And I will hunt ye: ye are in love, I know it:
Ye are an ass, and all the Camp shall know it.
A peevish idle boy; your Dame shall know it;
A wronger of my care; your self shall know it.

[Enter **CORPORAL JUDAS** and four **SOLDIERS**.

JUDAS
A Bean? a Princely diet, a full Banquet,
To what we compass.

1ST SOLDIER
Fight like Hogs for Acorns?

2ND SOLDIER
Venture our lives for Pig-nuts?

PETILLIUS
What ail these Rascals?

3RD SOLDIER
If this hold, we are starv'd.

JUDAS
For my part, friends,
Which is but twenty Beans a day, a hard world
For Officers, and men of action;
And those so clipt by master Mouse, and rotten:
For understand 'em French Beans, where the fruits
Are ripen'd like the people in old tubs.
For mine own part, I say, I am starv'd already.
Not worth another Bean, consum'd to nothing,
Nothing but flesh and bones left, miserable:
Now if this mustie provender can prick me
To honourable matters of atchievment, Gentlemen,
Why there's the point.

4TH SOLDIER
I'll fight no more.

PETILLIUS
You'll hang then,
A sovereign help for hunger. Ye eating Rascals,
Whose gods are Beef and Brewis, whose brave angers
Do execution upon these, and Chibbals:
Ye dogs heads i'th' porridge-pot; you fight no more?
Does Rome depend upon your resolution
For eating mouldy Pie-crust?

3RD SOLDIER
Would we had it.

JUDAS

I may do service, Captain.

PETILLIUS
In a fish-market.
You, Corporal Curry-Comb, what will your fighting
Profit the Common-wealth? do you hope to triumph,
Or dare your vamping valour, goodman Cobler,
Clap a new soal to th' Kingdom? s'death, ye dog-whelps
You, fight, or not fight.

JUDAS
Captain.

PETILLIUS
Out, ye flesh-flies,
Nothing but noise and nastiness.

JUDAS
Give us meat,
Whereby we may do.

PETILLIUS
Whereby hangs your valour?

JUDAS
Good bits afford good blows.

PETILLIUS
A good position:
How long is't since thou eat'st last, wipe thy mouth,
And then tell truth.

JUDAS
I have not eat to th' purpose—

PETILLIUS
To th' purpose? what's that? half a Cow and Garlick?
Ye Rogues, my company eat Turf, and talk not;
Timber they can digest, and fight upon't;
Old matts, and mud with spoons, rare meats. Your shooes slaves?
Dare ye cry out for hunger, and those extant?
Suck your Sword-hilts, ye slaves, if ye be valiant,
Honor will make 'em march-pain: to the purpose?
A grievous penance. Dost thou see that Gentleman,
That melancholly Monsieur?

JUNIUS
Pray ye, Petillius.

PETILLIUS
He has not eat these three weeks.

2ND SOLDIER
'Has drunk the more then.

3RD SOLDIER
And that's all one.

PETILLIUS
Nor drunk nor slept these two months.

JUDAS
Captain, we do beseech you as poor Soldiers,
Men that have seen good days, whose mortal stomachs
May sometime feel afflictions.

JUNIUS
This, Petillius,
Is not so nobly done.

PETILLIUS
'Tis common profit;
Urge him to th' point, he'll find you out a food
That needs no teeth nor stomach; a strange furmity
Will feed ye up as fat as hens i'th' foreheads,
And make ye fight like Fichocks, to him.

JUDAS
Captain.

JUNIUS
Do you long to have your throats cut?

PETILLIUS
See what metal
It makes in him: two meals more of this melancholly,
And there lies Caratach.

JUDAS
We do beseech ye.

2ND SOLDIER
Humbly beseech your valour.

JUNIUS
Am I only

Become your sport Petillius?

JUDAS
But to render
In way of general good, in preservation.

JUNIUS
Out of my thoughts, ye slaves.

4TH SOLDIER
Or rather pity.

3RD SOLDIER
Your warlike remedy against the maw-worms.

JUDAS
Or notable receipt to live by nothing.

PETILLIUS
Out with your Table-books.

JUNIUS
Is this true friendship?
And must my killing-griefs make others May-games?
Stand from my swords point, slaves, your poor starv'd spirits
Can make me no oblations; else, O love,
Thou proudly blind destruction, I would send thee
Whole Hecatombs of hearts, to bleed my sorrows.

JUDAS
Alas, he lives by love, Sir.

[Exit **JUNIUS**.

PETILLIUS
So he does, Sir,
And cannot you do so too? All my Company
Are now in love, ne'r think of meat, nor talk
Of what Provant is: Aymees, and Hearty hey-hoes,
Are Sallets fit for Soldiers. Live by meat;
By larding up your bodies? 'tis lewd, and lazie,
And shews ye meerly mortal, dull, and drives ye
To fight like Camels, with baskets at your noses.
Get ye in love; ye can whore well enough,
That all the world knows: fast ye into Famine,
Yet ye can crawl like Crabs to wenches, handsomely,
Fall but in love now, as ye see example,
And follow it but with all your thoughts, probatum,

There's so much charge sav'd, and your hunger's ended.
Away, I hear the General: get ye in love all,

[Drum afar off.

Up to the ears in love, that I may hear
No more of these rude murmurings; and discreetly
Carry your stomachs, or I prophesie
A pickel'd Rope will choak ye. Jog, and talk not.

[Exeunt.

[Enter **SWETONIUS**, **DEMETRIUS**, **DECIUS**, Drum, Colours.

SWETONIUS
Demetrius, is the messenger dispatch'd
To Penyus, to command him to bring up
The Volans Regiment?

DEMETRIUS
He's there by this time.

SWETONIUS
And are the Horse well view'd we brought from Mona.

DECIUS
The Troops are full, and lusty.

SWETONIUS
Good Petillius,
Look to those eating Rogues, that bawl for victuals,
And stop their throats a day or two: provision
Waits but the wind to reach us.

PETILLIUS
Sir, already
I have been tampring with their stomachs, which I find
As deaf as Adders to delays: your clemency
Hath made their murmurs, mutinies, nay, rebellions:
Now, and they want but Mustard, they'r in uproars
No oil but Candy, Lusitanian Figs
And Wine from Lesbos now can satisfie 'em:
The British waters are grown dull and muddy,
The fruit disgustful: Orontes must be sought for,
And Apples from the happy Isles: the truth is,
They are more curious now in having nothing,
Than if the sea and land turn'd up their treasures:
This lost the Colonies, and gave Bonduca

(With shame we must record it) time and strength
To look into our Fortunes; great discretion
To follow offered Victory; and last, full pride
To brave us to our teeth, and scorn our ruines.

SWETONIUS
Nay, chide not, good Petillius, I confess
My will to conquer Mona, and long stay
To execute that Will, let in these losses:
All shall be right again, and as a Pine
Rent from Oeta by a sweeping tempest,
Joynted again, and made a Mast, defies
Those angry winds that split him: so will I,
Piec'd to my never-failing strength and fortune,
Steer thorow these swelling dangers; plow their prides up,
And bear like thunder through their loudest tempests:
They keep the field still.

DEMETRIUS
Confident and full.

PETILLIUS
In such a number, one would swear they grew,
The hills are wooded with their partisans,
And all the valleys overgrown with darts,
As moors are with rank rushes: no ground left us
To charge upon, no room to strike: say fortune
And our endeavours bring us in to 'em,
They are so infinite, so ever-springing.
We shall be kill'd with killing; of desperate Women,
That neither fear, or shame e'r found, the devil
Has rank'd amongst 'em multitudes: say the men fail,
They'll poison us with their petticoats: say they fail,
They have priests enough to pray us into nothing.

SWETONIUS
These are imaginations, dreams of nothing,
The man that doubts or fears.

DECIUS
I am free of both.

DEMETRIUS
The self-same I.

PETILLIUS
And I as free as any;
As careless of my flesh, of that we call life,

So I may lose it nobly; as indifferent
As if it were my diet. Yet, noble General,
It was a wisdom learn'd from you; I learn'd it,
And worthy of a Soldiers care, most worthy,
To weigh with most deliberate circumstance
The ends of accidents, above their offers;
How to go on and get, to save a Roman,
Whose one life is more worth in way of doing,
Than millions of these painted wasps; how viewing
To find advantage out; how; how, found, to follow it
With counsel and discretion, lest meer fortune
Should claim the victory.

SWETONIUS
'Tis true, Petillius,
And worthily remembred: the rule's certain,
Their uses no less excellent: but where time
Cuts off occasions, danger, time and all
Tend to a present peril, 'tis required
Our Swords and Manhoods be best counsellors,
Our expeditions, presidents. To win, is nothing,
Where reason, time and counsel are our Camp-masters:
But there to bear the field, then to be conquerors,
Where pale destruction takes us, takes us beaten,
In wants, and mutinies, our selves but handfuls,
And to our selves, our own fears, needs a new way,
A sudden and a desperate execution:
Here, how to save, is loss; to be wise, dangerous;
Only a present well-united strength,
And minds made up for all attempts, dispatch it:
Disputing and delay here, cools the courage;
Necessity gives time for doubts; things infinite,
According to the spirit they are preach'd to,
Rewards like them; and names for after-ages,
Must steel the Soldier; his own shame help to arm him;
And having forc'd his spirit, e'r he cools,
Fling him upon his enemies; sudden and swift,
Like Tigers amongst Foxes, we must fight for't:
Fury must be our Fortune; shame we have lost,
Spurs ever in our sides to prick us forward:
There is no other wisdom nor discretion
Due to this day of ruine, but destruction;
The Soldiers order first, and then his anger.

DEMETRIUS
No doubt they dare redeem all.

SWETONIUS

Then no doubt
The day must needs be ours. That the proud Woman
Is infinite in number, better likes me,
Than if we dealt with squadrons: half her Army
Shall choak themselves, their own swords dig their graves.
I'll tell ye all my fears, one single valour,
The virtues of the valiant Caratach
More doubts me than all Britain: he's a Soldier
So forg'd out, and so temper'd for great fortunes,
So much man thrust into him, so old in dangers,
So fortunate in all attempts, that his mere name
Fights in a thousand men, himself in millions,
To make him Roman. But no more. Petillius,
How stands your charge?

PETILLIUS
Ready for all employments,
To be commanded too, Sir.

SWETONIUS
'Tis well govern'd;
To morrow we'll draw out, and view the Cohorts:
I' th' mean time, all apply their offices.
Where's Junius?

PETILLIUS
In's Cabin,
Sick o'th' mumps, Sir.

SWETONIUS
How?

PETILLIUS
In love, indeed in love, most lamentably loving,
To the tune of Queen Dido.

DECIUS
Alas poor Gentleman.

SWETONIUS
'Twill make him fight the nobler. With what Lady?
I'll be a spokesman for him.

PETILLIUS
You'll scant speed, Sir.

SWETONIUS
Who is't?

PETILLIUS
The devil's dam, Bonduca's daughter,
Her youngest, crackt i'th' ring.

SWETONIUS
I am sorry for him:
But sure his own discretion will reclaim him,
He must deserve our anger else. Good Captains,
Apply your selves in all the pleasing forms
Ye can, unto the Soldiers; fire their spirits,
And set 'em fit to run this action;
Mine own provision shall be shar'd amongst 'em,
Till more come in: tell 'em, if now they conquer,
The fat of all the kingdom lies before 'em.
Their shames forgot, their honors infinite,
And want for ever banisht. Two days hence,
Our fortunes, and our swords, and gods be for us.

[Exeunt.

ACTUS SECUNDUS

SCÆNA PRIMA

Enter **PENYUS, REGULUS, MACER, DRUSIUS**.

PENYUS
I must come?

MACER
So the General commands, Sir.

PENYUS
I must bring up my Regiment?

MACER
Believe, Sir,
I bring no lye.

PENYUS
But did he say, I must come?

MACER
So delivered.

PENYUS
How long is't, Regulus, since I commanded
In Britain here?

REGULUS
About five years, great Penyus.

PENYUS
The General some five months. Are all my actions
So poor, and lost, my services so barren,
That I'm remembred in no nobler language
But Must come up?

MACER
I do beseech ye, Sir,
Weigh but the times estate.

PENYUS
Yes, good Lieutenant,
I do, and his that sways it. Must come up;
Am I turn'd bare Centurion? Must, and shall,
Fit Embasses to court my honor?

MACER
Sir—

PENYUS
Set me to lead a handful of my men
Against an hundred thousand barbarous slaves
That have marcht name by name with Romes best doers?
Serve 'em up some other meat; I'll bring no food
To stop the jaws of all those hungry wolfs.
My Regiment's mine own. I must, my language.

[Enter **CURIUS**.

CURIUS
Penyus, where lies the Host?

PENYUS
Where fate may find 'em.

CURIUS
Are they ingirt?

PENYUS
The Battel's lost.

CURIUS

So soon?

PENYUS

No; but 'tis lost, because it must be won:
The Britains must be Victors. Who e'r saw
A troop of bloody vultures hovering
About a few corrupted carcasses,
Let him behold the silly Roman host,
Girded with millions of fierce Britains Swains,
With deaths as many as they have had hopes;
And then go thither, he that loves his shame;
I scorn my life, yet dare not lose my name.

CURIUS

Do not you hold it a most famous end,
When both our names and lives are sacrific'd
For Romes increase?

PENYUS

Yes, Curius; but mark this too;
What glory is there, or what lasting Fame
Can be to Rome or us? what full example,
When one is smother'd with a multitude,
And crouded in amongst a nameless press?
Honor got out of Flint, and on their heads
Whose virtues, like the Sun, exhal'd all valours,
Must not be lost in mists and fogs of people,
Noteless, and out of name, but rude and naked:
Nor can Rome task us with impossibilities,
Or bid us fight against a flood: we serve her,
That she may proudly say she has good soldiers,
Not slaves to choak all hazards. Who but fools,
That make no difference betwixt certain dying,
And dying well, would fling their Fames and Fortunes
Into this Britain-gulf, this quick-sand ruine,
That sinking, swallows us, What noble hand
Can find a subject fit for blood there? or what sword
Room for his execution? What air to cool us,
But poison'd with their blasting breaths and curses,
Where we lie buried quick above the ground,
And are with labouring sweat, and breathless pain,
Kill'd like to slaves, and cannot kill again?

DRUSIUS

Penyus, mark antient Wars, and know that then
Captains weigh'd an hundred thousand men.

PENYUS

Drusius, mark antient wisdom, and you'll find then,
He gave the overthrow that sav'd his men,
I must not go.

REGULUS

The soldiers are desirous,
Their Eagles all drawn out, Sir.

PENYUS

Who drew up, Regulus?
Ha? speak: did you whose bold Will durst attempt this?
Drawn out? why, who commands, Sir? on whose warrant
Durst they advance?

REGULUS

I keep mine own obedience.

DRUSIUS

'Tis like the general cause, their love of honor,
Relieving of their wants.

PENYUS

Without my knowledge?
Am I no more? my place but at their pleasures?
Come, who did this?

DRUSIUS

By—Sir, I am ignorant.

[Drum softly within; then enter **SOLDIERS** with Drum and Colours.

PENYUS

What am I grown a shadow? Harke, they march.
I will know, and will be my self. Stand, disobedience;
He that advances one foot higher, dies for't.
Run thorow the Regiment upon your duties,
And charge 'em on command: beat back again,
By—I'll ti'th'em all else.

REGULUS

We'll do our best.

[Exeunt **DRUSIUS** and **REGULUS**.

PENYUS

Back; cease your bawling Drums there,
I'll beat the Tubs about your brains else. Back:

Do I speak with less fear than Thunder to ye?
Must I stand to beseech ye? home, home: ha?
Do ye stare upon me? Are those minds I moulded,
Those honest valiant tempers I was proud
To be a fellow to, those great discretions
Made your names fear'd and honor'd, turn'd to wild-fires?
O gods, to disobedience? Command, farewel:
And be ye witness with me, all things sacred,
I have no share in these mens shames. March, Soldiers,
And seek your own sad ruines; your old Penyus
Dares not behold your murders.

1ST SOLDIER
Captain.

2ND SOLDIER
Captain.

3RD SOLDIER
Dear honour'd Captain.

PENYUS
Too too dear lov'd Soldiers,
Which made ye weary of me: and Heaven yet knows,
Though in your mutinies, I dare not hate you;
Take your own Wills; 'tis fit your long experience
Should now know how to rule your selves: I wrong ye,
In wishing ye to save your lives and credits,
To keep your necks whole from the Ax hangs o'r ye:
Alas, I much dishonour'd ye: go, seek the Britains,
And say ye come to glut their sacrifices;
But do not say I sent ye. What ye have been,
How excellent in all parts, good, and govern'd,
Is only left of my Command, for story;
What now ye are, for pitie. Fare ye well.

[Enter **DRUSIUS** and **REGULUS**.

DRUSIUS
Oh turn again, great Penyus; see the Soldier
In all points apt for duty.

REGULUS
See his sorrow
For his disobedience, which he says was haste,
And haste (he thought) to please you with. See Captain,
The toughness of his courage turn'd to water;
See how his manly heart melts.

PENYUS
Go, beat homeward,
There learn to eat your little with obedience,
And henceforth strive to do as I direct ye.

[Exeunt **SOLDIERS**.

MACER
My answer, Sir.

PENYUS
Tell the Great General
My Companies are no fagots to fill breaches;
My self no man that must, or shall, can carry:
Bid him be wise; and where he is, he's safe then;
And when he finds out possibilities,
He may command me. Commend me to the Captains.

MACER
All this I shall deliver.

PENYUS
Farewel, Macer.

[Exit **PENYUS**.

CURIUS
Pray gods this breed no mischief.

REGULUS
It must needs,
If stout Suetonius win; for then his anger,
Besides the Soldiers loss of due, and honor,
Will break together on him.

DRUSIUS
He's a brave fellow;
And but a little hide his haughtiness,
(Which is but sometimes neither, on some causes)
He shews the worthiest Roman this day living.
You may, good Curius, to the General
Make all things seem the best.

CURIUS
I shall endeavour:
Pray for our fortunes, Gentlemen, If we fall,
This one farewel serves for a Funeral.

The gods make sharp our swords, and steel our hearts;
We dare, alas, but cannot fight our parts.

[Exeunt.

SCÆNA SECUNDA

Enter **JUNIUS**, **PETILLIUS** and a **HERALD** observing Junius.

PETILLIUS
Let him go on: stay, now he talks.

JUNIUS
Why?
Why should I love mine enemie? what is beauty?
Of what strange violence, that like the plague,
It works upon our spirits? blind they feign him,
I am sure, I find it so.

PETILLIUS
A Dog shall lead ye.

JUNIUS
His fond affections blinder.

PETILLIUS
Hold ye there still.

JUNIUS
It takes away my sleep.

PETILLIUS
Alas, poor chicken.

JUNIUS
My company, content; almost my fashion.

PETILLIUS
Yes, and your weight too, if you follow it.

JUNIUS
'Tis sure the plague, for no man dare come near me
Without an Antidote: 'tis far worse; Hell.

PETILLIUS
Thou art damn'd without redemption then.

JUNIUS

The way to't
Strew'd with fair Western smiles, and April blushes,
Led by the brightest constellations; eyes,
And sweet proportions, envying heaven: but from thence
No way to guide, no path, no wisdom bring us.

PETILLIUS

Yes, a smart water, Junius.

JUNIUS

Do I fool?
Know all this, and fool still? Do I know further,
That when we have enjoy'd our ends, we lose 'em,
And all our appetites are but as dreams
We laugh at in our ages.

PETILLIUS

Sweet Philosopher!

JUNIUS

Do I know on still, and yet know nothing? Mercy gods,
Why am I thus ridiculous?

PETILLIUS

Motley on thee,
Thou art an arrant Ass.

JUNIUS

Can red and white,
An Eye, a Nose, a Cheek.

PETILLIUS

But one cheek, Junius?
An half-fac'd Mistriss?

JUNIUS

With a little trim,
That wanton fools call Fashion, thus abuse me?
Take me beyond my reason? Why should not I
Doat on my horse well trapt, my sword well hatch'd?
They are as handsome things, to me more useful,
And possible to rule too. Did I but love,
Yet 'twere excusable, my youth would bear it;
But to love there, and that no time can give me,
Mine honor dare not ask: she has been ravish'd
My nature must not know; she hates our Nation.

Thus to dispose my spirit!

PETILLIUS
Stay a little,
He will declaim again.

JUNIUS
I will not love; I am a man, have reason,
And I will use it: I'll no more tormenting,
Nor whining for a wench, there are a thousand.

PETILLIUS
Hold thee there boy.

JUNIUS
A thousand will intreat me.

PETILLIUS
Ten thousand, Junius.

JUNIUS
I am young and lusty,
And to my fashion valiant; can please nightly.

PETILLIUS
I'll swear thy back's probatum, for I have known thee
Leap at sixteen like a strong Stallion.

JUNIUS
I will be man again.

PETILLIUS
Now mark the working,
The devil and the spirit tug for't: twenty pound
Upon the devils head.

JUNIUS
I must be wretched.

PETILLIUS
I knew I had won.

JUNIUS
Nor have I so much power
To shun my fortune.

PETILLIUS
I will hunt thy fortune

With all the shapes imagination breeds,

[Musick.

But I will fright thy devil: Stay, he sings now.

SONG, by **JUNIUS** and **PETILLIUS**, after him in mockage.

JUNIUS
Must I be thus abus'd?

PETILLIUS
Yes marry must ye.
Let's follow him close: oh, there he is, now read it.

HERALD [reads]
It is the Generals command, that all sick, persons old and unable, retire within the Trenches; he that fears his liberty, to leave the Field: Fools, Boys, and Lovers must not come near the Regiments, for fear of their infections; especially those Cowards they call Lovers.

JUNIUS
Ha?

PETILLIUS
Read on.

HERALD
If any common Soldier love an enemy, he's whip'd and made a slave: If any Captain, cast, with loss of honors, flung out o'th' Army, and made unable ever after to bear the name of a Soldier.

JUNIUS
The—consume ye all, Rogues.

[Exit **JUNIUS**.

PETILLIUS
Let this work:
H'as something now to chew upon: he's gone,
Come, shake no more.

HERALD
Well, Sir, you may command me,
But not to do the like again for Europe;
I would have given my life for a bent two-pence.
If I e'r read to Lovers whilst I live again,
Or come within their confines—

PETILLIUS

There's your payment,
And keep this private.

HERALD
I am school'd for talking.

[Exit **HERALD**.

[Enter **DEMETRIUS**.

PETILLIUS
How now, Demetrius, are we drawn?

DEMETRIUS
'Tis doing:
Your Company stands fair; but pray ye, where's Junius?
Half his command are wanting, with some forty
That Decius leads.

PETILLIUS
Hunting for Victuals:
Upon my life free-booting Rogues, their stomachs
Are like a widows lust, ne'r satisfied.

DEMETRIUS
I wonder how they dare stir, knowing the enemy
Master of all the Countrey.

PETILLIUS
Resolute hungers
Know neither fears nor faiths, they tread on ladders,
Ropes, Gallows, and overdoe all dangers.

DEMETRIUS
They may be hang'd though.

PETILLIUS
There's their joyful supper,
And no doubt they are at it.

DEMETRIUS
But for heavens sake,
How does young Junius?

PETILLIUS
Drawing on, poor Gentleman.

DEMETRIUS

What, to his end?

PETILLIUS
To th' end of all flesh: woman.

DEMETRIUS
This Love has made him a stout Soldier.

PETILLIUS
O, a great one,
Fit to command young Goslings: but what news?

DEMETRIUS
I think the messengers come back from Penyus,
By this time, let's go know.

PETILLIUS
What will you say now
If he deny to come, and take exceptions
At some half syllable, or sound deliver'd
With an ill accent, or some stile left out?

DEMETRIUS
I cannot think he dare.

PETILLIUS
He dare speak treason,
Dare say, what no man dares believe, dares do—But
that's all one: I'll lay you my black armor
To twenty crowns, he comes not.

DEMETRIUS
Done.

PETILLIUS
You'll pay.

DEMETRIUS
I will.

PETILLIUS
Then keep thine old use Penyus,
Be stubborn and vain glorious, and I thank thee.
Come let's go pray for six hours: most of us
I fear will trouble heaven no more: two good blows
Struck home at two Commanders of the Britains,
And my part's done.

DEMETRIUS
I do not think of dying.

PETILLIUS
'Tis possible we may live. But Demetrius,
With what strange legs, and arms, and eyes, and noses,
Let Carpenters and Copper-smiths consider.
If I can keep my heart whole, and my wind-pipe,
That I may drink yet like a Soldier—

DEMETRIUS
Come, let's have better thoughts; mine's on your Armour.

PETILLIUS
Mine's in your purse, Sir; Let's go try the wager.

[Exeunt.

SCÆNIA TERTIA

Enter **JUDAS** and his four **COMPANIONS** (halters about their necks) **BONDUCA**, her **DAUGHTERS**,
NENNIUS following.

BONDUCA
Come, hang 'em presently.

NENNIUS
What made your Rogueships
Harrying for victuals here? Are we your friends;
Or do you come for Spies? tell me directly,
Would you not willingly be hang'd now? do not ye long for't?

JUDAS
What say ye? shall we hang in this vain? Hang we must
And 'tis as good to dispatch it merrily,
As pull an arse like dogs to't.

1ST SOLDIER
Any way,
So it be handsome.

3RD SOLDIER
I had as lief 'twere toothsome too: but all agree,
And I'll not out Boys.

4TH SOLDIER

Let's hang pleasantly.

JUDAS
Then pleasantly be it: Captain, the truth is,
We had as lief hang with meat in our mouths,
As ask your pardon empty.

BONDUCA
These are brave hungers.
What say you to a leg of Beef now, sirrah?

JUDAS
Bring me acquainted with it, and I'll tell ye.

BONDUCA
Torment 'em wenches: I must back; then hang 'em.

JUDAS
We humbly thank your Grace.

1ST DAUGHTER
The Rogues laugh at us.

2ND DAUGHTER
Sirrah, What think you of a wench now?

JUDAS
A wench, Lady?
I do beseech your Ladyship, retire.
I'll tell ye presently, ye see the time's short;
One crash; even to the setling of my conscience.

NENNIUS
Why, is't no more but up, boys?

JUDAS
Yes, ride too Captain
Will you but see my seat?

1ST DAUGHTER
Ye shall be set, Sir,
Upon a jade shall shake ye.

JUDAS
Sheets, good Madam,
Will do it ten times better.

1ST DAUGHTER

Whips, good Soldier.
Which ye shall taste before ye hang, to mortifie ye;
'Tis pity ye should die thus desperate.

2ND DAUGHTER
These are the merry Romans the brave madcaps.
'Tis ten to one we'll cool your resolutions.
Bring out the whips.

JUDAS
Would your good Ladyships
Would exercise 'em too.

4TH SOLDIER
Surely Ladies,
We'll shew you a strange patience.

NENNIUS
Hang 'em Rascals,
They'll talk thus on the wheel.

[Enter **CARATACH**.

CARATACH
Now, what's the matter?
What are these fellows? what's the crime committed,
That they wear necklaces?

NENNIUS
They are Roman Rogues,
Taken a Forraging.

CARATACH
Is that all, Nennius?

JUDAS
Would I were fairly hang'd; this is the devil,
The kill-cow, Caratach,

CARATACH
And you would hang 'em.

NENNIUS
Are they not enemies?

1ST SOLDIER
My breech makes buttons.

1ˢᵀ DAUGHTER
Are they not our tormentors?

CARATACH
Tormentors? Flea-traps.
Pluck off your halters, fellows.

NENNIUS
Take heed, Caratach,
Taint not your wisdom.

CARATACH
Wisdom, Nennius?
Why, who shall fight against us, make our honors,
And give a glorious day into our hands,
If we dispatch our foes thus? what's their offence?
Stealing a loaf or two to keep out hunger,
A piece of greazie bacon, or a pudding?
Do these deserve the gallows, they are hungry,
Poor hungry knaves, no meat at home left, starv'd:
Art thou not hungry?

JUDAS
Monstrous hungry.

CARATACH
He looks like hungers self: get 'em some victuals,
And Wine to cheer their hearts, quick: Hang up poor pilchers?

2ᴺᴰ SOLDIER
This is the bravest Captain—

NENNIUS
Caratach,
I'll leave you to your Will.

CARATACH
I'll answer all, Sir.

2ᴺᴰ DAUGHTER
Let's up and view his entertainment of 'em.
I am glad they are shifted any way, their tongues else
Would still have murdred us.

1ˢᵀ DAUGHTER
Let's up and see it.

[Exeunt.

[Enter **HENGO**.

CARATACH
Sit down poor knaves: why where's this Wine and Victuals?
Who waits there?

SWETONIUS
within. Sir, 'tis coming.

HENGO
Who are these Uncle?

CARATACH
They are Romans, boy.

HENGO
Are these they
That vex mine Aunt so? can these fight? they look
Like empty scabbards, all, no mettle in 'em,
Like men of clouts, set to keep crows from orchards;
Why, I dare fight with these.

CARATACH
That's my good chicken. And how do ye?
How do you feel your stomachs?

JUDAS
Wondrous apt, Sir,
As shall appear when time calls.

CARATACH
That's well, down wi'th't,
A little grace will serve your turns: eat softly,
You'll choak ye knaves else: give 'em Wine.

JUDAS
Not yet, Sir,
We're even a little busie.

HENGO
Can that fellow
Do any thing but eat? thou fellow.

JUDAS
Away boy,
Away, this is no boys play.

HENGO
By—, Uncle,
If his valour lie in's teeth, he's the most valiant.

CARATACH
I am glad to hear ye talk, Sir,

HENGO
Good Uncle tell me,
What's the price of a couple of cramm'd Romans?

CARATACH
Some twenty Britains boy; these are good Soldiers,

HENGO
Do not the cowards eat hard too?

CARATACH
No more, boy.
Come, I'll sit with you too; sit down by me, boy.

JUDAS
Pray bring your dish then.

CARATACH
Hearty knaves: More meat there.

1ST SOLDIER
That's a good hearing.

CARATACH
Stay now and pledge me.

JUDAS
This little piece, Sir.

CARATACH
By—square eaters,
More meat I say: upon my conscience
The poor Rogues have not eat this month: how terribly
They charge upon their victuals: dare ye fight thus?

JUDAS
Believe it, Sir, like devils.

CARATACH
Well said famine,
Here's to thy General.

JUDAS
Most excellent Captain, I will now pledg thee.

CARATACH
And to morrow night say to him,
His Head is mine.

JUDAS
I can assure ye Captain,
He will not give it for this washing.

CARATACH
Well said.

[**DAUGHTERS** above.

1ST DAUGHTER
Here's a strange entertainment: how the thieves drink.

2ND DAUGHTER
Danger is dry, they look'd for colder liquor.

CARATACH
Fill 'em more wine, give 'em full bowls; which of you all now
In recompence of this good, dare but give me
A sound knock in the battel?

JUDAS
Delicate Captain,
To do thee a sufficient recompence,
I'll knock thy brains out.

CARATACH
Do it.

HENGO
Thou dar'st as well be damn'd: thou knock his brains out.
Thou skin of man? Uncle, I will not hear this.

JUDAS
Tie up your whelp.

HENGO
Thou kill my Uncle?
Would I had but a sword for thy sake, thou dry'd dog.

CARATACH

What a mettle
This little vermin carries.

HENGO
Kill mine Uncle?

CARATACH
He shall not, child.

HENGO
He cannot: he's a Rogue,
An only eating Rogue: Kill my sweet Uncle?
Oh that I were a man.

JUDAS
By this Wine,
Which I will drink to Captain Junius,
Who loves the Queens most excellent Majesties little daughter
Most sweetly, and most fearfully I will do it.

HENGO
Uncle, I'll kill him with a great pin.

CARATACH
No more, Boy.
I'll pledge thy Captain: To ye all good fellows.

2ND DAUGHTER
In love with me? that love shall cost your lives all:
Come Sister, and advise me; I have here
A way to make an easie conquest of 'em,
If fortune favour me.

CARATACH
Let's see ye sweat
To morrow, blood and spirit, Boys, this Wine
Turn'd to stern valour.

1ST SOLDIER
Hark ye Judas,
If he should hang us after all this.

JUDAS
Let him:
I'll hang like a Gentleman and a Roman.

CARATACH
Take away there,

They have enough.

JUDAS
Captain, we thank you heartily
For your good cheer, and if we meet to morrow,
One of us pays for't.

CARATACH
Get 'em guides, their Wine
Has over-master'd 'em.

[Enter **2ND DAUGHTER** and a **SERVANT**.

2ND DAUGHTER
That hungry fellow
With the red beard there, give it him, and this,
To see it well delivered.

CARATACH
Farewel knaves;
Speak nobly of us, keep your words to morrow.

[Enter a **GUIDE**.

And do something worthy your meat. Go, guide 'em,
And see 'em fairly onward.

JUDAS
Meaning me, Sir?

SERVANT
The same.
The youngest daughter to the Queen intreats ye
To give this privately to Captain Junius,
This for your pains.

JUDAS
I rest her humble servant,
Commend me to thy Lady. Keep your Files, boys.

SERVANT
I must instruct ye farther.

JUDAS
Keep your Files there.
Order, sweet friends: faces about now.

GUIDE

Here Sir,
Here lies your way.

JUDAS
'Bless the Founders, I say,
Fairly, good soldiers, fairly march now: close, boys.

[Exeunt.

SCÆNA QUARTA

Enter **SWETONIUS, PETILLIUS, DEMETRIUS, DECIUS, MACER.**

SWETONIUS
Bid me be wise, and keep me where I am,
And so be safe: not come, because commanded;
Was it not thus?

MACER
It was, Sir.

PETILLIUS
What now think ye?

SWETONIUS
Must come, so hainous to him, so distasteful?

PETILLIUS
Give me my money.

DEMETRIUS
I confess 'tis due, Sir,
And presently I'll pay it.

SWETONIUS
His obedience.
So blind at his years and experience,
It cannot find where to be tendred?

MACER
Sir,
The Regiment was willing, and advanc'd too,
The Captains at all points steel'd up: their preparations
Full of resolve, and confidence; Youth and fire,
Like the fair breaking of a glorious day,
Guilded their Phalanx: when the angry Penyus

Stept like a stormy cloud 'twixt them and hopes.

SWETONIUS
And stopt their resolutions?

MACER
True: his reason
To them was ods, and ods so infinite,
Discretion durst not look upon.

SWETONIUS
Well Penyus,
I cannot think thee coward yet; and treacherous
I dare not think: thou hast lopt a limb off from me,
And let it be thy glory, thou wast stubborn,
Thy wisdom, that thou leftst thy General naked:
Yet e'r the Sun set, I shall make thee see,
All valour dwels not in thee; all command
In one experience. Thou wilt too late repent this,
And wish, I must come up, had been thy blessing.

PETILLIUS
Let's force him.

SWETONIUS
No, by no means; he's a torrent
We cannot easily stemme.

PETILLIUS
I think, a Traitor.

SWETONIUS
No ill words: let his own shame first revile him.
That Wine I have, see it (Demetrius)
Distributed amongst the soldiers,
To make 'em high and lusty: when that's done,
Petillius, give the word through, that the Eagles
May presently advance: no man discover,
Upon his life, the enemies full strength,
But make it of no value: Decius,
Are your starv'd people yet come home?

DECIUS
I hope so.

SWETONIUS
Keep 'em in more obedience: This is no time
To chide, I could be angry else, and say more to ye:

But come, let's order all: whose sword is sharpest,
And valour equal to his sword this day,
Shall be my Saint.

PETILLIUS
We shall be holy all then.

[Exeunt.

[Enter **JUDAS** and his **COMPANY**.

JUDAS
Captain, Captain, I have brought 'em off again;
The drunkennest slaves.

DECIUS
—Confound your Rogueships;
I'll call the General, and have ye hang'd all.

JUDAS
Pray who will you command then?

DECIUS
For you, sirrah,
That are the ring-leader to these devises,
Whose maw is never cramm'd, I'll have an engine.

JUDAS
A wench, sweet Captain.

DECIUS
Sweet Judas, even the Forks.
Where ye shall have two Lictors with two whips
Hammer your hide.

JUDAS
Captain, good words, fair words,
Sweet words, good Captain; if you like not us,
Farewell, we have imployment.

DECIUS
Where hast thou been?

JUDAS
There where you dare not be with all your valour.

DECIUS
Where's that?

JUDAS
With the best good fellow living.

1ˢᵀ SOLDIER
The king of all good fellows.

DECIUS
Who's that?

JUDAS
Caratach.
Shake now, and say, We have done something worthy,
Mark me; with Caratach: By this—Caratach:
Do you as much now and you dare: sweet Caratach.
Ye talk of a good fellow, of true drinking;
Well, go thy waies old Caratach: besides the drink Captain,
The bravest running Banquet of black puddings,
Pieces of glorious beef.

DECIUS
How scap'd ye hanging?

JUDAS
Hanging's a dog's death, we are Gentlemen,
And I say still, old Caratach.

DECIUS
Belike then,
You are turn'd Rebels all.

JUDAS
We are Roman boys all,
And boys of mettle: I must do that Captain,
This day, this very day.

DECIUS
Away, ye Rascal.

JUDAS
Fair words, I say again.

DECIUS
What must you do, Sir?

JUDAS
I must do that my heart-strings yern to do:
But my word's past.

DECIUS
What is it?

JUDAS
Why, kill Caratach.
That's all he ask'd us for our entertainment.

DECIUS
More than you'll pay.

JUDAS
Would I had sold my self
Unto the skin I had not promis'd it:
For such another Caratach—

DECIUS
Come Fool,
Have ye done your Countrey service?

JUDAS
I have brought that
To Captain Junius.

DECIUS
How?

JUDAS
I think will do all:
I cannot tell, I think so.

DECIUS
How? to Junius?
I'll more enquire of this: You'll fight now?

JUDAS
Promise:
Take heed of promise, Captain.

DECIUS
Away, and rank then.

JUDAS
But harke ye Captain, there is Wine distributing,
I would fain know what share I have.

DECIUS
Be gone,

Ye have too much.

JUDAS
Captain, no Wine, no fighting.
There's one call'd Caratach that has Wine.

DECIUS
Well, Sir,
If you'll be rul'd now, and do well.

JUDAS
Do excellent.

DECIUS
Ye shall have Wine, or any thing: go file;
I'll see ye have your share: drag out your dormise,
And stow 'em somewhere, where they may sleep handsomly,
They'l hear a hunt's up shortly.

JUDAS
Now I love thee:
But no more Forks nor Whips.

DECIUS
Deserve 'em not then:
Up with your men, I'll meet ye presently;
And get 'em sober quickly.

JUDAS
Arm, arm, Bullies;
All's right again and straight; and which is more,
More Wine, more Wine: Awake ye men of Memphis,
Be sober and discreet, we have much to do boys.

[Exeunt.

ACTUS TERTIUS

SCÆNA PRIMA

Enter a **MESSENGER**.

MESSENGER
Prepare there for the sacrifice, the Queen comes.

[Musick.

[Enter in solemnity the **DRUIDS** singing, the **2ND DAUGHTER** strewing Flowers: then **BONDUCA**, **NENNIUS** and **OTHERS**.

BONDUCA
Ye powerful gods of Britain, hear our prayers;
Hear us you great Revengers, and this day
Take pity from our swords, doubt from our valours,
Double the sad remembrance of our wrongs
In every brest; the vengeance due to those
Make infinite and endless: on our pikes
This day pale terror sit, horrors and ruines
Upon our executions; claps of thunder
Hang on our armed carts, and 'fore our Troops
Despair and death; shame beyond these attend 'em.
Rise from the dust, ye relicks of the dead,
Whose noble deeds our holy Druids sing,
Oh rise, ye valiant bones, let not base earth
Oppress your honors, whilst the pride of Rome
Treads on your Stocks, and wipes out all your stories.

NENNIUS
Thou great Tiranes, whom our sacred Priests,
Armed with dreadful thunder, plac'd on high
Above the rest of the immortal gods,
Send thy consuming fires, and deadly bolts,
And shoot 'em home, stick in each Roman heart
A fear fit for confusion; blast their spirits,
Dwell in 'em to destruction; thorow their Phalanx
Strike, as thou strik'st a proud tree; shake their Bodies,
Make their strengths totter, and their topless fortunes
Unroot and reel to ruine.

1ST DAUGHTER
O thou god,
Thou feared god, if ever to thy justice
Insulting wrongs, and ravishments of Women,
Women deriv'd from thee, their shames, the sufferings
Of those that daily fill'd thy Sacrifice
With virgin incense, have access, now hear me,
Now snatch thy thunder up, now on these Romans,
Despisers of thy power, of us defacers,
Revenge thy self, take to thy killing anger,
To make thy great work full, thy justice spoken,
An utter rooting from this blessed Isle
Of what Rome is or has been.

BONDUCA

Give more incense,
The gods are deaf and drowsie; no happy flame
Rises to raise our thoughts: Pour on.

2ND DAUGHTER

See heaven,
And all you pow'rs that guide us, see, and shame
We kneel so long for pity over your Altars;
Since 'tis no light oblation that you look for,
No incense offering, will I hang mine eyes;
And as I wear these stones with hourly weeping,
So will I melt your pow'rs into compassion.
This tear for Prosutagus my brave Father,
Ye gods, now think on Rome; this for my Mother,
And all her miseries; yet see, and save us;
But now ye must be open-ey'd. See; heaven,
Oh see thy show'rs stoln from thee; our dishonours,

[A smoak from the Altar.

Oh Sister, our dishonors: can ye be gods,
And these sins smother'd?

BONDUCA

The fire takes.

CARATACH

It does so,
But no flame rises. Cease your fearful prayers,
Your whinings, and your tame petitions;
The gods love courage arm'd with confidence,
And prayers fit to pull them down: weak tears
And troubled hearts, the dull twins of cold spirits,
They sit and smile at. Hear how I salute 'em:
Divine Andate, thou who hold'st the reins
Of furious Battels, and disordred War,
And proudly roll'st thy swarty chariot wheels
Over the heaps of wounds and carcasses,
Sailing through seas of blood; thou sure-steel'd sternness,
Give us this day good hearts, good enemies,
Good blowes o' both sides, wounds that fear or flight
Can claim no share in; steel us both with angers,
And warlike executions fit thy viewing;
Let Rome put on her best strength, and thy Britain,
Thy little Britain, but as great in fortune,
Meet her as strong as she, as proud, as daring;
And then look on, thou red ey'd god: who does best,
Reward with honor; who despair makes flie,

Unarm for ever, and brand with infamy:
Grant this, divine Andate, 'tis but justice;
And my first blow thus on thy holy Altar

[A flame arises.

I sacrifice unto thee.

BONDUCA
It flames out.

[Musick.

CARATACH
Now sing ye Druides.

[Song.

BONDUCA
'Tis out again.

CARATACH
H'as given us leave to fight yet; we ask no more,
The rest hangs in our resolutions:
Tempt her no more.

BONDUCA
I would know farther Cosen.

CARATACH
Her hidden meaning dwels in our endeavors;
Our valors are our best gods. Cheer the Soldier,
And let him eat.

MESSENGER
He's at it, Sir.

CARATACH
Away then;
When he has done, let's march. Come, fear not Lady,
This day the Roman gains no more ground here,
But what his body lies in.

BONDUCA
Now I am confident.

[Exeunt **RECORDERS**.

SCÆNA SECUNDA

Enter **JUNIUS, CURIUS, DECIUS**.

DECIUS
We dare not hazard it: beside our lives,
It forfeits all our understandings.

JUNIUS
Gentlemen,
Can ye forsake me in so just a service,
A service for the Common-wealth, for honor?
Read but the Letter; you may love too.

DECIUS
Read it:
If there be any safety in the circumstance,
Or likelihood 'tis love, we will not fail ye.
Read it good Curius.

CURIUS
Willingly.

JUNIUS
Now mark it.

CURIUS
reads. Health to thy heart, my honoured Junius,
And all thy love requited: I am thine,
Thine everlastingly, thy love has won me,
And let it breed no doubt; our new acquaintance
Compels this, 'tis the gods decree to bless us.
The times are dangerous to meet; yet fail not,
By all the love thou bear'st me I conjure thee,
Without distrust of danger, to come to me,
For I have purpos'd a delivery
Both of my self and fortune this blest day
Into thy hands, if thou thinkst good: to shew thee
How infinite my Love is, even my Mother
Shall be thy prisoner, the day yours without hazard;
For I beheld your danger like a Lover,
A just affecter of thy faith: Thy goodness,
I know, will use us nobly, and our Marriage
If not redeem, yet lessen Romes Ambition.
I'm weary of these miseries: Use my Mother,
(if you intend to take her) with all honour,

And let this disobedience to my parents
Be laid on love, not me. Bring with thee, Junius,
Spirits resolv'd to fetch me off, the noblest,
Forty will serve the turn; just at the joyning
Of both the battels, we will be weakly guarded;
And for a guide, within this hour shall reach thee
A faithful friend of mine: the gods, my Junius,
Keep thee, and me to serve thee: young Bonvica.

CURIUS
This letter carries much belief, and most objections
Answer'd, we must have doubted.

DECIUS
Is that fellow
Come to ye for a guide yet?

JUNIUS
Yes.

DECIUS
And examin'd?

JUNIUS
Far more then that; he has felt tortures, yet
He vows he knows no more than this truth.

DECIUS
Strange.

CURIUS
If she mean what she writes, as't may be probable,
'Twill be the happiest vantage we can lean to.

JUNIUS
I'll pawn my soul she means truth.

DECIUS
Think an hour more,
Then If your confidence grow stronger on ye,
We'll set in with ye.

JUNIUS
Nobly done; I thank ye;
Ye know the time.

CURIUS
We will be either ready

To give ye present counsell, or joyn with ye.

[Enter **SWETONIUS**, **PETILLIUS** and **DEMETRIUS**, **MACER**.

JUNIUS
No more as ye are Gentlemen. The general.

SWETONIUS
Draw out apace, the enemy waits for us;
Are ye all ready?

JUNIUS
All our Troops attend, Sir.

SWETONIUS
I am glad to hear you say so, Junius.
I hope ye are dispossest.

JUNIUS
I hope so too, Sir.

SWETONIUS
Continue so. And Gentlemen, to you now;
To bid you fight is needless, ye are Romans,
The name will fight it self; To tell ye who
You go to fight against, his power, and nature,
But loss of time: ye know it, know it poor,
And oft have made it so. To tell ye farther,
His Body shows more dreadful than it has done,
To him that fears, less possible to deal with,
Is but to stick more honor on your actions,
Load ye with virtuous names, and to your memories
Tye never dying time, and fortune constant.
Go on in full assurance, draw your swords
As daring and as confident as justice;
The gods of Rome fight for ye; loud Fame calls ye,
Pitch'd on the topless Apenine, and blows
To all the under world: all Nations,
The seas, and unfrequented deserts, where the snow dwels,
Wakens the ruin'd monuments, and there
Where nothing but eternal death and sleep is,
Informs again the dead bones. With your virtues,
Go on, I say, valiant and wise, rule heaven,
And all the great aspects attend 'em. Do but blow
Upon this enemy, who, but that we want foes,
Cannot deserve that name; and like a myst,
A lazie fog, before your burning valors
You'll find him fly to nothing, This is all,

We have swords, and are the sons of antient Romans,
Heirs to their endless valors, fight and conquer.

DEMETRIUS
'Tis done.

PETILLIUS
That man that loves not this day,
And hugs not in his arms the noble danger,
May he dye fameless and forgot.

SWETONIUS
Sufficient,
Up to your Troops, and let your drums beat thunder,
March close, and sudden like a tempest: all executions

[March.

Done without sparkling of the Body: keep your phalanx
Sure lin'd, and piec'd together; your pikes forward,
And so march like a moving Fort: ere this day run,
We shall have ground to add to Rome, well won.

[Exeunt.

SCÆNA TERTIA

Enter **CARATACH** and **NENNIUS**.

NENNIUS
The Roman is advanc'd from yound' hills brow,
We may behold him, Caratach.

[A March.

[Drums within at one place afar off.

CARATACH
Let's thither,
I see the dust flie. Now I see the body,
Observe 'em, Nennius, by—a handsome Body,
And of a few, strongly and wisely joynted:
Swetonius is a Souldier.

NENNIUS
As I take it,

That's he that gallops by the Regiments,
Viewing their preparations.

CARATACH
Very likely,
He shews no less than General: see how bravely
The Body moves, and in the head how proudly
The Captains stick like plumes: he comes apace on;
Good Nennius go, and bid my stout Lieutenant
Bring on the first square Body to oppose 'em,
And as he charges, open to inclose 'em:
The Queen move next with hers, and wheel about,
To gain their backs, in which I'll lead the Vantguard.
We shall have bloody crowns this day, I see by't;
Hast thee good Nennius, I'll follow instantly.

[Exit **NENNIUS**.

How close they march, as if they grew together!

[March.

No place but lin'd alike: sure from oppression;
They will not change this figure: we must charge 'em,
And charge 'em home at both ends, Van and Rere,

[Drums in another place afar off.

They never totter else. I hear our Musick,
And must attend it: Hold good sword, but this day,
And bite hard where I hound thee, and hereafter
I'll make a relique of thee, for young Souldiers
To come like Pilgrimes to, and kiss for Conquests.

[Exit.

SCÆNA QUARTA

Enter **JUNIUS**, **CURIUS**, and **DECIUS**.

JUNIUS
Now is the time, the fellow stays.

DECIUS
What think ye?

CURIUS
I think 'tis true.

JUNIUS
Alas, if 'twere a question,
If any doubt or hazzard fell into't,
Do ye think mine own discretion so self-blind,
My care of you so naked, to run headlong?

DECIUS
Let's take Petillius with us.

JUNIUS
By no means:
He's never wise but to himself, nor courteous,
But where the end's his own: we are strong enough,
If not too many. Behind yonder hill
The fellow tells me she attends, weak guarded,
Her Mother and her Sister.

CARATACH
I would venture.

JUNIUS
We shall not strike five blows for't, weigh the good,
The general good may come.

DECIUS
Away, I'll with ye,
But with what doubt?

JUNIUS
Fear not, my soul for all.

[Exeunt.

[Alarms, Drums and Trumpets in several places afar off, as at a main Battell.

SCÆNA QUINTA

Enter **DRUSIUS** and **PENYUS** above.

DRUSIUS
Here ye may see 'em all, Sir; from this hill
The Country shews off levell.

PENYUS

Gods defend me,
What multitudes they are, what infinites!
The Roman power shews like a little Star
Hedg'd with a double hollo. Now the knell rings,

[Loud shouts.

Heark how they shout to th' battel; how the air
Totters and reels, and rends apieces, Drusus,
With the huge vollied clamours.

DRUSIUS

Now they charge.
Oh gods, of all sides, fearfully.

PENYUS

Little Rome,
Stand but this growing Hydra one short hour,
And thou hast out-done Hercules.

DRUSIUS

The dust hides 'em,
We cannot see what follows.

PENYUS

They are gone,
Gone, swallow'd, Drusus, this eternal Sun
Shall never see 'em march more.

DRUSIUS

O turn this way,
And see a modell of the field, some forty,
Against four hundred.

PENYUS

Well fought, bravely follow'd;
O nobly charg'd again, charg'd home too: Drusus,
They seem to carry it: now they charge all,

[Loud shouts.

Close, close, I say; they follow it: ye gods,
Can there be more in men? more daring spirits?
Still they make good their fortunes. Now they are gone too,
For ever gone: see Drusus at their backs
A fearful Ambush rises. Farewell valours,
Excellent valours: O Rome, where's thy wisdome?

DRUSIUS
They are gone indeed, Sir.

PENYUS
Look out toward the Army,
I am heavy with these slaughters.

DRUSIUS
'Tis the same still,
Covered with dust and fury.

[Enter the two **DAUGHTERS**, with **JUNIUS**, **CURIUS**, **DECIUS** and **SOLDIERS**.

2ND DAUGHTER
Bring 'em in,
Tie 'em, and then unarm 'em.

1ST DAUGHTER
Valiant Romans,
Ye are welcome to your Loves.

2ND DAUGHTER
Your death, fools.

DECIUS
We deserve 'em,
And women do your worst.

1ST DAUGHTER
Ye need not beg it.

2ND DAUGHTER
Which is kind Junius?

SERVANT
This.

2ND DAUGHTER
Are you my sweet heart?
It looks ill on't: how long is't, pretty soul,
Since you and I first lov'd? Had we not reason
To doat extreamly upon one another?
How does my Love? this is not he: my chicken
Could prate finely, sing a love-song.

JUNIUS
Monster.

2ND DAUGHTER
Oh, now it courts.

JUNIUS
Arm'd with more malice
Then he that got thee has the divell.

2ND DAUGHTER
Good.
Proceed, sweet chick.

JUNIUS
I hate thee, that's my last.

2ND DAUGHTER
Nay, and ye love me, forward: No? Come sister,
Let's prick our answers on our arrows points,
And make 'em laugh a little. Ye damn'd Leachers,
Ye proud improvident fools, have we now caught ye?
Are ye i'th' noose? Since ye are such loving creatures,
We'll be your Cupids: Do ye see these arrows?
We'll send them to your wanton livers, goats.

1ST DAUGHTER
O how I'll trample on your hearts, ye villains,
Ambitious salt-itch slaves: Romes master sins,
The mountain Rams topt your hot mothers.

2ND DAUGHTER
Dogs,
To whose brave founders a salt whore gave suck;
Theeves, honors hangmen, do ye grin? perdition
Take me for ever, if in my fell anger,

[Enter **CARATACH**.

I do not out-do all example.

CARATACH
Where,
Where are these Ladies? ye keep noble quarter,
Your Mother thinks ye dead or taken; upon which,
She will not move her Battel. Sure these faces
I have beheld and known, they are Roman Leaders,
How came they here?

2ND DAUGHTER

A trick Sir, that we us'd,
A certain policy conducted 'em
Unto our snare: we have done ye no small service;
These us'd as we intend, we are for th' battel,

CARATACH
As you intend? taken by treachery?

1ST DAUGHTER
Is't not allow'd?

CARATACH
Those that should gild our Conquest,
Make up a Battel worthy of our winning,
Catch'd up by craft?

2ND DAUGHTER
By any means that's lawful.

CARATACH
A womans wisdom in our triumphs? out,
Out ye sluts, ye follies; from our swords
Filch our revenges basely? arm again, Gentlemen:
Soldiers, I charge ye help 'em.

2ND DAUGHTER
By—Uncle,
We will have vengeance for our rapes.

CARATACH
By—
You should have kept your legs close then: dispatch there.

1ST DAUGHTER
I will not off thus.

CARATACH
He that stirs to execute,
Or she, though it be your selves, by him that got me,
Shall quickly feel mine anger. one great day given us,
Not to be snatch'd out of our hands but basely;
And we must shame the gods from whence we have it,
With setting snares for Soldiers? I'll run away first,
Be hooted at, and children call me coward,
Before I set up scales for Victories:
Give 'em their swords.

2ND DAUGHTER

O gods.

CARATACH
Bear off the women
Unto their Mother.

2ND DAUGHTER
One shot, gentle Uncle.

CARATACH
One cut her fiddle-string: Bear 'em off I say.

1ST DAUGHTER
The—take this fortune.

CARATACH
Learn to spin,
And curse your knotted hemp: go Gentlemen,

[Exeunt **DAUGHTERS**.

Safely go off, up to your Troops: be wiser,
There thank me like tall Soldiers: I shall seek ye.

[Exit **CARATACH**.

CURIUS
A noble worth.

DECIUS
Well Junius.

JUNIUS
Pray ye no more.

CURIUS
He blushes, do not load him.

DECIUS
Where's your love now?

[Drums loud again.

JUNIUS
Puffe, there it flies: Come, let's redeem our follies.

[Exeunt **JUNIUS**, **CURIUS**, **DECIUS**.

DRUSIUS
Awake, Sir; yet the Roman Bodie's whole,
I see 'em clear again.

PENYUS
Whole? 'tis not possible:
Drusus they must be lost.

DRUSIUS
By—they are whole, Sir,
And in brave doing; see, they wheel about
To gain more ground.

PENYUS
But see there, Drusus, see,
See that huge Battel moving from the mountains,
Their gilt coats shine like Dragons scales, their march
Like a rough tumbling storm; see them, and view 'em,
And then see Rome no more: say they fail; look,
Look where the armed carts stand; a new Army:
Look how they hang like falling rocks, as murdring
Death rides in triumph Drusus: fell destruction
Lashes his fiery horse, and round about him
His many thousand ways to let out souls.
Move me again when they charge, when the mountain
Melts under their hot wheels, and from their Ax'trees
Huge claps of thunder plough the ground before 'em,
Till then I'll dream what Rome was.

[Enter **SWETONIUS, PETILLIUS, DEMETRIUS, MACER.**

SWETONIUS
O bravely fought; honor till now nere show'd
Her golden face i'th' field. Like Lions, Gentlemen,
Y'have held your heads up this day: Where's young Junius,
Curius and Decius?

PETILLIUS
Gone to heaven, I think, Sir.

SWETONIUS
Their worths go with 'em: breathe a while: How do ye?

PETILLIUS
Well; some few scurvy wounds, my heart's whole yet.

DEMETRIUS
Would they would give us more ground.

SWETONIUS
Give? we'll have it.

PETILLIUS
Have it? and hold it too, despight the devill.

[Enter **JUNIUS, DECIUS, CURIUS.**

JUNIUS
Lead up to th' head, and line: sure the Qs. Battell
Begins to charge like wild-fire: where's the General?

SWETONIUS
Oh, they are living yet. Come my brave soldiers,
Come, let me pour Romes blessing on ye; Live,
Live, and lead Armies all: ye bleed hard.

JUNIUS
Best:
We shall appear the sterner to the foe.

DECIUS
More wounds, more honor.

PETILLIUS
Lose no time.

SWETONIUS
Away then,
And stand this shock, ye have stood the world.

PETILLIUS
Wee'll grow to't.
Is not this better than lowsie loving?

JUNIUS
I am my self, Petillius.

PETILLIUS
'Tis I love thee.

[Exeunt **ROMANS.**

[Enter **BONDUCA, CARATACH, DAUGHTERS, NENNIUS.**

CARATACH
Charge 'em i'th' flanks: O ye have plaid the fool,

The fool extreamly, the mad fool.

BONDUCA
Why Cosin?

CARATACH
The woman fool. Why did you give the word
Unto the carts to charge down, and our people
In gross before the Enemy? we pay for't,
Our own swords cut our throats: why?—on't;
Why do you offer to command? the divell,
The divell, and his dam too, who bid you
Meddle in mens affairs?

[Exeunt **QUEEN**, &c.

BONDUCA
I'll help all.

CARATACH
Home,
Home and spin woman, spin, go spin, ye trifle.
Open before there, or all's ruine. How,

[Shouts within.

Now comes the Tempest; on our selves, by—

WITHIN
Victoria.

CARATACH
O woman, scurvie woman, beastly woman.

[Exeunt.

DRUSIUS
Victoria, Victoria.

PENYUS
How's that, Drusus?

DRUSIUS
They win, they win, they win; oh look, look, look, Sir,
For heavens sake look, the Britains fly, the Britains fly.
Victoria.

[Enter **SWETONIUS**, **SOLDIERS** and **CAPTAINS**.

SWETONIUS
Soft, soft, pursue it soft; excellent Soldiers,
Close, my brave fellows, honorable Romans:
Oh cool thy mettle Junius, they are ours,
The world cannot redeem 'em: stern Petillius,
Govern the conquest nobly: soft, good Soldiers.

[Exeunt.

[Enter **BONDUCA, DAUGHTERS** and **BRITONS**.

BONDUCA
Shame, whither flie ye, ye unlucky Britains?
Will ye creep into your mothers wombs again? Back cowards.
Hares, fearful Hares, Doves in your angers; leave me?
Leave your Queen desolate? her hapless children.

[Enter **CARATACH** and **HENGO**.

To Roman rape again and fury?

CARATACH
Flye, ye buzzards,
Ye have wings enough, ye fear: get thee gone, woman,

[Loud shout within.

Shame tread upon thy heels; all's lost, all's lost, heark,
Heark how the Romans ring our knels.

[Exit **BONDUCA**, &c.

HENGO
Good Uncle,
Let me go too.

CARATACH
No boy, thy fortune's mine,
I must not leave thee; get behind me; shake not,

[Enter **PETILLIUS, JUNIUS, DECIUS**.

I'll breech ye, if ye do boy: Come, brave Romans,
All is not lost yet.

JUNIUS
Now I'll thank thee, Caratach.

[Fight. Drums.

CARATACH
Thou art a Soldier: strike home, home, have at ye.

PENYUS
His blows fall like huge sledges on an anvil.

DECIUS
I am weary.

PETILLIUS
So am I.

CARATACH
Send more swords to me.

JUNIUS
Let's sit and rest.

[Sit down.

DRUSIUS
What think ye now?

PENYUS
O Drusus,
I have lost mine honor, lost my name,
Lost all that was my light: these are true Romans,
And I a Britain coward, a base Coward;
Guide me where nothing is but desolation,
That I may never more behold the face
Of Man, or Mankind know me: O blind Fortune,
Hast thou abus'd me thus?

DRUSIUS
Good Sir, be comforted;
It was your wisdom rul'd ye; pray ye go home,
Your day Is yet to come, when this great fortune
Shall be but foil unto it.

[Retreat.

PENYUS
Fool, fool, Coward.

[Exit **PENYUS** and **DRUSIUS**.

[Enter **SWETONIUS**, **DEMETRIUS**, **SOLDIERS**, Drum and Colours.

SWETONIUS
Draw in, draw in: well have you fought, and worthy
Romes noble recompence; look to your wounds,
The ground is cold and hurtful: the proud Queen
Has got a Fort, and there she and her Daughters
Defie us once again. To morrow morning
Wee'll seek her out, and make her know, our Fortunes
Stop at no stubborn walls: Come, sons of honor,
True virtues heirs; thus hatch'd with Britain blood,
Let's march to rest, and set in gules like Suns.
Beat a soft march, and each one ease his neighbours.

[Exeunt.

ACTUS QUARTUS

SCÆNA PRIMA

Enter **PETILLIUS**, **JUNIUS**, **DECIUS**, **DEMETRIUS** singing.

PETILLIUS
Smooth was his cheek,

DECIUS
And his chin it was sleek,

JUNIUS
With whoop, he has done wooing.

DEMETRIUS
Junius was this Captains name,
A lad for a lasses viewing,

PETILLIUS
Full black his eye, and plump his thigh,

DECIUS
Made up for loves pursuing:

DEMETRIUS
Smooth was his cheeck,

PETILLIUS

And his chin it was sleek,

JUNIUS
With whoop, he has done wooing.

PETILLIUS
O my vex'd thief, art thou come home again?
Are thy brains perfect?

JUNIUS
Sound as bels.

PETILLIUS
Thy back-worm
Quiet, and cast his sting, boy?

JUNIUS
Dead, Petillius,
Dead to all folly, and now my anger only.

PETILLIUS
Why, that's well said: hang Cupid and his quiver,
A drunken brawling Boy; thy honour'd saint
Be thy ten shillings, Junius, there's the money,
And there's the ware; square dealing: this but sweats thee
Like a Mesh nag, and makes thee look pin buttock'd;
The other runs thee whining up and down
Like a pig in a storm, fills thy brains full of madness,
And shews thee like a long Lent, thy brave body
Turn'd to a tail of green-fish without butter.

DECIUS
When thou lov'st next, love a good cup of Wine,
A Mistress for a King, she leaps to kiss thee,
Her red and white's her own; she makes good blood,
Takes none away; what she heats sleep can help,
Without a groping Surgeon.

JUNIUS
I am counsell'd,
And henceforth, when I doat again,—

DEMETRIUS
Take heed,
Ye had almost paid for't.

PETILLIUS
Love no more great Ladies,

Thou canst not step amiss then; there's no delight in 'em;
All's in the whistling of their snacht up silks;
They're only made for handsome view, not handling;
Their bodies of so weak and wash a temper,
A rough pac'd bed will shake 'em all to pieces;
A tough hen pulls their teeth out, tyres their souls;
Plenæ rimarum sunt, they are full of rynnet,
And take the skin off where they are tasted; shun 'em,
They live in cullisses like rotten cocks
Stew'd to a tenderness, that holds no tack:
Give me a thing I may crush.

JUNIUS
Thou speak'st truly:
The Wars shall be my Mistriss now.

PETILLIUS
Well chosen,
For she's a bownsing lass, she'll kiss thee at night, boy,
And break thy pate i'th' morning.

JUNIUS
Yesterday
I found those favors infinite.

DEMETRIUS
Wench good enough,
But that she talks too loud.

PETILLIUS
She talks to th' purpose,
Which never Woman did yet: she'll hold grapling,
And he that layes on best, is her best servant:
All other loves are meer catching of dotrels,
Stretching of legs out only, and trim laziness.
Here comes the General.

[Enter **SWETONIUS**, **CURIUS** & **MACER**.

SWETONIUS
I am glad I have found ye:
Are those come in yet that pursu'd bold Caratach?

PETILLIUS
Not yet Sir, for I think they mean to lodge him;
Take him I know they dare not, 'twill be dangerous.

SWETONIUS

Then haste Petillius, haste to Penyus,
I fear the strong conceit of what disgrace
Has pull'd upon himself, will be his ruine:
I fear his soldiers fury too; haste presently,
I would not lose him for all Britain. Give him, Petillius.

PETILLIUS
That that shall choak him.

SWETONIUS
All the noble counsell,
His fault forgiven too, his place, his honor,

PETILLIUS
For me, I think, as handsome.

SWETONIUS
All the comfort.
And tell the Soldier, 'twas on our command
He drew not to the Battell.

PETILLIUS
I conceive Sir,
And will do that shall cure all.

SWETONIUS
Bring him with ye
Before the Queens Fort, and his Forces with him,
There you shall find us following of our Conquest:
Make haste.

PETILLIUS
The best I may.

[Exit.

SWETONIUS
And noble Gentlemen,
Up to your Companies: we'll presently
Upon the Queens pursult: there's nothing done
Till she be seiz'd; without her nothing won.

[Exeunt.

[Short flourish.

SCÆNIA SECUNDA

Enter **CARATACH** and **HENGO**.

CARATACH
How does my Boy?

HENGO
I would do well, my heart's well;
I do not fear.

CARATACH
My good Boy.

HENGO
I know, Uncle,
We must all dye; my little brother dy'd,
I saw him dye, and he dy'd smiling: sure,
There's no great pain in't Uncle. But pray tell me,
Whither must we go when we are dead?

CARATACH
Strange questions!
Why, to the blessed'st place Boy: ever sweetness
And happiness dwells there.

HENGO
Will you come to me?

CARATACH
Yes, my sweet boy.

HENGO
Mine Aunt too, and my Cosins?

CARATACH
All, my good child.

HENGO
No Romans, Uncle?

CARATACH
No Boy.

HENGO
I should be loath to meet them there.

CARATACH

No ill men,
That live by violence, and strong oppression,
Come thither: 'tis for those the gods love, good men.

HENGO
Why, then I care not when I go; for surely
I am perswaded they love me: I never
Blasphem'd 'em, Uncle, nor transgrest my parents;
I always said my Prayers.

CARATACH
Thou shalt go then,
Indeed thou shalt.

HENGO
When they please.

CARATACH
That's my good boy.
Art thou not weary, Hengo?

HENGO
Weary, Uncle?
I have heard you say you have march'd all day in Armour.

CARATACH
I have, boy.

HENGO
Am not I your Kinsman?

CARATACH
Yes.

HENGO
And am not I as fully allyed unto you
In those brave things, as blood?

CARATACH
Thou art too tender.

HENGO
To go upon my legs? they were made to bear me.
I can play twenty mile a day, I see no reason
But to preserve my Countrey and my self,
I should march forty.

CARATACH

What, wouldst thou be
Living to wear a mans strength?

HENGO
Why a Caratach,
A Roman-hater, a scourge sent from Heaven

[Drum.

To whip these proud theeves from our Kingdom. Heark,
Heark, Uncle, heark, I hear a Drum.

[Enter **JUDAS** and his **PEOPLE** to the door.

JUDAS
Beat softly,
Softly, I say; they are here: who dare charge?

1ST SOLDIER
He
That dares be knockt o'th' head: I'll not come near him.

JUDAS
Retire again, and watch then. How he stares!
H'as eyes would kill a dragon: mark the boy well;
If we could take or kill him. A—on ye,
How fierce ye look! see how he broods the boy;
The devil dwels in's scabbard. Back, I say,
Apace, apace, h'as found us.

[They retire.

CARATACH
Do ye hunt us?

HENGO
Uncle, good Uncle see, the thin starv'd Rascal,
The eating Roman, see where he thrids the thickets:
Kill him, dear Uncle, kill him; one good blow
To knock his brains into his breech; strike's head off,
That I may piss in's face.

CARATACH
Do ye make us Foxes?
Here, hold my charging staff, and keep the place boy.
I'am at bay, and like a bull I'll bear me.
Stand, stand, ye Rogues, ye Squirrels.

[Exit.

HENGO
Now he pays 'em:
O that I had a mans strength.

[Enter **JUDAS**, &c.

JUDAS
Here's the boy;
Mine own, I thank my Fortune.

HENGO
Uncle, uncle;
Famine is faln upon me, uncle.

JUDAS
Come, Sir,
Yield willingly, your Uncle's out of hearing,
I'll ticle your young tail else.

HENGO
I defie thee,
Thou mock-made man of mat: charge home, sirha:
Hang thee, base slave, thou shak'st.

JUDAS
Upon my conscience
The boy will beat me: how it looks, how bravely,
How confident the worm is: a scabb'd boy
To handle me thus? yield or I cut thy head off.

HENGO
Thou dar'st not cut my finger: here't is, touch it.

JUDAS
The boy speaks sword and buckler, Prethee yield, boy:
Come, here's an apple, yield.

HENGO
By—he fears me.
I'll give you sharper language: When, ye coward,
When come ye up?

JUDAS
If he should beat me—

HENGO

When, Sir?
I long to kill thee; come, thou can'st not scape me.
I have twenty ways to charge thee; twenty deaths
Attend my bloody staff.

JUDAS
Sure 'tis the devil,
A dwarf, devil in a doublet.

HENGO
I have kill'd a Captain, sirha, a brave Captain,
And when I have done, I have kickt him thus. Look here,
See how I charge this staff.

JUDAS
Most certain
This boy will cut my throat yet.

[Enter **TWO SOLDIERS** running.

1ST SOLDIER
Flee, flee, he kills us.

2ND SOLDIER
He comes, he comes.

JUDAS
The devil take the hindmost.

HENGO
Run, run, ye Rogues, ye precious Rogues, ye rank Rogues.
A comes, a comes, a comes, a comes: that's he, boys.
What a brave cry they make!

[Enter **CARATACH** with a head.

CARATACH
How does my chicken?

HENGO
'Faith, uncle, grown a Soldier, a great Soldier;
For by the virtue of your charging-staff,
And a strange fighting face I put upon't,
I have out-brav'd hunger.

CARATACH
That's my boy, my sweet boy.
Here, here's a Roman's head for thee.

HENGO

Good provision.
Before I starve, my sweet-fac'd Gentleman,
I'll trie your favour.

CARATACH

A right compleat Soldier.
Come, chicken, let's go seek some place of strength
(The Countrey's full of Scouts) to rest a while in,
Thou wilt not else be able to endure
The journey to my Countrey, fruits, and water,
Must be your food a while, boy.

HENGO

Any thing:
I can eat moss, I can live on anger,
To vex these Romans. Let's be wary, Uncle.

CARATACH

I warrant thee; come chearfully.

HENGO

And boldly.

SCÆNA TERTIA

Enter **PENYUS**, **DRUSIUS** and **REGULUS**.

REGULUS

The soldier shall not grieve ye.

PENYUS

Pray ye forsake me;
Look not upon me, as ye love your Honors;
I am so cold a coward, my infection
Will choke your virtues like a damp else.

DRUSIUS

Dear Captain.

REGULUS

Most honour'd Sir.

PENYUS

Most hated, most abhor'd;

Say so, and then ye know me, nay, ye please me.
O my dear credit, my dear credit.

REGULUS
Sure
His mind is dangerous.

DRUSIUS
The good gods cure it.

PENYUS
My honour got thorow fire, thorow stubborn breaches
Thorow Battels that have been as hard to win as heaven,
Thorow death himself, in all his horrid trims,
Is gone for ever, ever, ever, Gentlemen,
And now I am left to scornful tales and laughters,
To hootings at, pointing with fingers, That's he,
That's the brave Gentleman forsook the battel,
The most wise Penyus, the disputing coward.
O my good sword, break from my side, and kill me;
Cut out the coward from my heart.

REGULUS
Ye are none.

PENYUS
He lyes that says so: by—he lyes, lyes basely,
Baser than I have done. Come, soldiers, seek me,
I have robb'd ye of your virtues: Justice, seek me,
I have broke my fair obedience, lost: shame take me,
Take me, and swallow me, make ballads of me;
Shame, endless shame: and pray do you forsake me.

DRUSIUS
What shall we do?

PENYUS
Good Gentlemen forsake me:
You were not wont to be commanded. Friends, pray do it,
And do not fear; for as I am a coward
I will not hurt my self: when that mind takes me,
I'll call to you, and ask your help. I dare not.

[Enter **PETILLIUS**.

PETILLIUS
Good morrow, Gentlemen; where's the Tribune?

REGULUS
There.

DRUSIUS
Whence come ye, good Petillius?

PETILLIUS
From the General.

DRUSIUS
With what, for heavens sake?

PETILLIUS
With good counsel, Drusus,
And love, to comfort him.

DRUSIUS
Good Regulus
Step to the Soldier, and allay his anger;
For he is wild as winter.

[Exeunt **DRUSIUS** and **REGULUS**.

PETILLIUS
O, are ye there? have at ye. Sure he's dead,
It cannot be he dare out-live this fortune:
He must die, 'tis most necessary; men expect it;
And thought of life in him, goes beyond coward.
Forsake the field so basely? fie upon't:
So poorly to betray his worth; so coldly
To cut all credit from the soldier? sure
If this man mean to live, as I should think it
Beyond belief, he must retire where never
The name of Rome, the voice of Arms, or Honour
Was known or heard of yet: he's certain dead,
Or strongly means it; he's no Soldier else,
No Roman in him; all he has done, but outside,
Fought either drunk or desperate. Now he rises.
How does Lord Penyus?

PENYUS
As ye see.

PETILLIUS
I am glad on't;
Continue so still. The Lord General,
The valiant General, great Swetonius—

PENYUS
No more of me is spoken; my name's perish'd.

PETILLIUS
He that commanded fortune and the day
By his own valour and discretion,
When, as some say, Penyus refused to come,
But I believe 'em not, sent me to see ye.

PENYUS
Ye are welcome; and pray see me; see me well,
Ye shall not see me long.

PETILLIUS
I hope so, Penyus;
The gods defend, Sir.

PENYUS
See me, and understand me: This is he
Left to fill up your triumph; he that basely
Whistled his honour off to th' wind; that coldly
Shrunk in his politick head, when Rome like reapers
Sweat blood, and spirit, for a glorious harvest,
And bound it up, and brought it off: that fool,
That having gold and copper offer'd him,
Refus'd the wealth, and took the wast: that soldier
That being courted by loud fame and fortune,
Labour in one hand, that propounds us gods,
And in the other, glory that creates us,
Yet durst doubt, and be damned.

PETILLIUS
It was an errour.

PENYUS
A foul one, and a black one.

PETILLIUS
Yet the blackest
May be washt white again.

PENYUS
Never.

PETILLIUS
Your leave, Sir,
And I beseech ye note me; for I love ye,
And bring along all comfort: Are we gods,

Alli'd to no infirmities? are our natures
More than mens natures? when we slip a little
Out of the way of virtue, are we lost?
Is there no medicine called Sweet mercy?

PENYUS
None, Petillius;
There is no mercy in mankind can reach me,
Nor is it fit it should; I have sinn'd beyond it.

PETILLIUS
Forgiveness meets with all faults.

PENYUS
'Tis all faults,
All sins I can commit, to be forgiven:
'Tis loss of whole man in me, my discretion
To be so stupid, to arrive at pardon.

PETILLIUS
O but the General—

PENYUS
He's a brave Gentleman,
A valiant, and a loving; and I dare say
He would, as far as honor durst direct him,
Make even with my fault, but 'tis not honest,
Nor in his power: examples that may nourish
Neglect and disobedience in whole bodies.
And totter the estates and faiths of armies,
Must not be plaid withall; nor out of pitty
Make a General forget his duty:
Nor dare I hope more from him than is worthy.

PETILLIUS
What would ye do?

PENYUS
Dye.

PETILLIUS
So would sullen children,
Women that want their wills, slaves, disobedient,
That fear the law, die. Fie, great Captain; you
A man to rule men, to have thousand lives
Under your Regiment, and let your passion
Betray your reason? I bring you all forgiveness,
The noblest kind commends, your place, your honour.

PENYUS

Prethee no more; 'tis foolish: didst not thou?
By—thou didst, I over-heard thee, there,
There where thou standst now, deliver me for rascal,
Poor, dead, cold coward, miserable, wretched,
If I out-liv'd this ruine?

PETILLIUS

I?

PENYUS

And thou didst it nobly,
Like a true man, a souldier: and I thank thee,
I thank thee, good Petillius; thus I thank thee.

PETILLIUS

Since ye are so justly made up, let me tell ye,
'Tis fit ye dye indeed.

PENYUS

O how thou lov'st me!

PETILLIUS

For say he had forgiven ye; say the peoples whispers
Were tame again, the time run out for wonder,
What must your own Command think, from whose Swords
Ye have taken off the edges, from whose valours
The due and recompence of Arms; nay, made it doubtful
Whether they knew obedience? must not these kill ye?
Say they are won to pardon ye, by meer miracle
Brought to forgive ye; what old valiant Souldier,
What man that loves to fight, and fight for Rome,
Will ever follow you more? dare ye know these ventures?
If so, I bring ye comfort; dare ye take it?

PENYUS

No, no, Petillius, no.

PETILLIUS

If your mind serve ye,
Ye may live still; but how? yet pardon me,
You may outwear all too, but when? and certain
There is a mercy for each fault, if tamely
A man will take't upon conditions.

PENYUS

No, by no means: I am only thinking now, Sir,

(For I am resolved to go) of a most base death,
Fitting the baseness of my fault. I'll hang.

PETILLIUS
Ye shall not; y'are a Gentleman I honor,
I would else flatter ye, and force ye live,
Which is far baser. Hanging? 'tis a dogs death,
An end for slaves.

PENYUS
The fitter for my baseness.

PETILLIUS
Besides, the man that's hang'd, preaches his end,
And sits a sign for all the world to gape at.

PENYUS
That's true: I'll take a fitter poison.

PETILLIUS
No,
'Tis equal ill; the death of rats and women,
Lovers, and lazie boys, that fear correction,
Die like a man.

PENYUS
Why my sword then.

PETILLIUS
I, If your Sword be sharp, Sir,
There's nothing under heaven that's like your Sword;
Your Sword's a death indeed.

PENYUS
It shall be sharp, Sir.

PETILLIUS
Why Mithridates was an arrant asse
To dye by poison, if all Bosphorus
Could lend him Swords: your Sword must do the deed:
'Tis shame to dye choak'd, fame to dye and bleed.

PENYUS
Thou hast confirmed me: and, my good Petillius,
Tell me no more I may live.

PETILLIUS
'Twas my Commission;

But now I see ye in a nobler way,
A way to make all even.

PENYUS
Fare-well, Captain:
Be a good man, and fight well: be obedient:
Command thy self, and then thy men. Why shakest thou?

PETILLIUS
I do not Sir.

PENYUS
I would thou hadst, Petillius:
I would find something to forsake the world with
Worthy the man that dies: a kind of earth-quake
Through all stern valors but mine own.

PETILLIUS
I feel now
A kind of trembling in me.

PENYUS
Keep it still,
As thou lov'st virtue, keep it.

PETILLIUS
And brave Captain,
The great and honoured Penyus.

PENYUS
That again:
O how it heightens me! again, Petillius.

PETILLIUS
Most excellent Commander.

PENYUS
Those were mine,
Mine, only mine.

PETILLIUS
They are still.

PENYUS
Then to keep 'em
For ever falling more, have at ye, heavens,
Ye everlasting powers, I am yours: The work's done,

[Kills himself.

That neither fire nor age, nor melting envy
Shall ever conquer. Carry my last words
To the great General: kiss his hands and say,
My soul I give to heaven, my fault to justice
Which I have done upon my self: my virtue,
If ever there was any in Poor Penyus,
Made more, and happier, light on him. I faint.
And where there is a foe, I wish him fortune.
I dye: lye lightly on my ashes, gentle earth.

PETILLIUS
And on my sin. Farewell, great Penyus,

[Noise within.

The souldier is in fury. Now I am glad
'Tis done before he comes. This way, for me,
The way of toile; for thee, the way of honor.

[Exit.

[Enter **DRUSUS** and **REGULUS** with **SOLDIERS**.

SOLDIERS
Kill him, kill him, kill him.

DRUSIUS
What will ye do?

REGULUS
Good soldiers, honest soldiers.

SOLDIERS
Kill him, kill him, kill him.

DRUSIUS
Kill us first; we command too.

REGULUS
Valiant Soldiers,
Consider but whose life ye seek. O Drusus,
Bid him be gone, he dies else. Shall Rome say
(Ye most approved Souldiers) her dear children
Devoured the fathers of the fights? shall rage
And stubborn fury guide those swords to slaughter,
To slaughter of their own, to civil ruine?

DRUSIUS

O let 'em in: all's done, all's ended, Regulus,
Penyus has found his last eclipse. Come, Souldiers,
Come, and behold your miseries: come bravely,
Full of your mutinous and bloody angers,
And here bestow your darts. O only Romane,
O father of the Wars.

REGULUS

Why stand ye stupid?
Where be your killing furies? whose sword now
Shall first be sheath'd in Penyus? do ye weep?
Howl out, ye wretches, ye have cause: howl ever.
Who shall now lead ye fortunate? whose valor
Preserve ye to the glory of your Countrey?
Who shall march out before ye, coy'd and courted
By all the Mistrisses of War, care, counsel,
Quick-ey'd experience, and victory twin'd to him?
Who shall beget ye deeds beyond inheritance
To speak your names, and keep your honors living,
When children faill, and time that takes all with him,
Build houses for ye to oblivion?

DRUSIUS

O ye poor desperate fools: no more now, souldiers;
Go home, and hang your arms up; let rust rot 'em;
And humble your stern valors to soft prayers;
For ye have sunk the frame of all your virtues;
The sun that warm'd your bloods is set for ever:
I'll kiss thy honor'd cheek. Farewell, great Penyus,
Thou thunder-bolt, farewell. Take up the body:
To morrow morning to the Camp convey it.
There to receive due Ceremonies. That eye
That blinds himself with weeping, gets most glory.

[Exeunt with a dead march.

SCÆNA QUARTA

Enter **SWETONIUS, JUNIUS, DECIUS, DEMETRIUS, CURIUS** and **SOLDIERS: BONDUCA**, two **DAUGHTERS**,
and **NENNIUS**, above. Drum and Colours.

SWETONIUS

Bring up the Catapults and shake the wall,
We will not be out-brav'd thus.

NENNIUS
Shake the earth,
Ye cannot shake our souls. Bring up your Rams,
And with their armed heads, make the Fort totter;
Ye do but rock us into death.

[Exit **NENNIUS**.

JUNIUS
See, Sir,
See the Icenian Queen in all her glory
From the strong battlements proudly appearing,
As if she meant to give us lashes.

DECIUS
Yeild, Queen.

BONDUCA
I am unacquainted with that language, Roman.

SWETONIUS
Yield honour'd Lady, and expect our mercy,

[Exit **DECIUS**.

We love thy nobleness.

BONDUCA
I thank ye, ye say well;
But mercy and love are sins in Rome and hell.

SWETONIUS
Ye cannot scape our strength; ye must yield, Lady,
Ye must adore and fear the power of Rome.

BONDUCA
If Rome be earthly, why should any knee
With bending adoration worship her?
She's vitious; and your partial selves confess,
Aspires the height of all impiety:
Therefore 'tis fitter I should reverence
The thatched houses where the Britains dwell
In careless mirth, where the blest houshold gods
See nought but chast and simple purity.
'Tis not high power that makes a place divine,
Nor that the men from gods derive their line.
But sacred thoughts in holy bosoms stor'd,

Make people noble, and the place ador'd.

SWETONIUS
Beat the wall deeper.

BONDUCA
Beat it to the center,
We will not sink one thought.

SWETONIUS
I'll make ye.

BONDUCA
No.

2ND DAUGHTER
O mother, these are fearful hours: speak gently.

[Enter **PETILLIUS**.

To these fierce men, they will afford ye pitty.

BONDUCA
Pitty? thou fearful girl; 'tis for those wretches
That misery makes tame. Wouldst thou live less?
Wast not thou born a Princess? Can my blood,
And thy brave fathers spirit, suffer in thee
So base a separation from thy self,
As mercy from these Tyrants? Thou lov'st lust sure,
And long'st to prostitute thy youth and beauty
To common slaves for bread. Say they had mercy;
The divel a relenting conscience:
The lives of Kings rest in their Diadems,
Which to their bodies lively souls do give,
And ceasing to be Kings, they cease to live.
Show such another fear, and—
I'll fling thee to their fury.

SWETONIUS
He is dead then?

PETILLIUS
I think so certainly; yet all my means, Sir,
Even to the hazzard of my life—

SWETONIUS
No more:
We must not seem to mourn here.

[Enter **DECIUS**.

DECIUS
There's a breach made,
Is it your will we charge, Sir?

SWETONIUS
Once more mercy,
Mercy to all that yield.

BONDUCA
I scorn to answer:
Speak to him girl; and hear thy Sister.

1ST DAUGHTER
General,
Hear me, and mark me well, and look upon me
Directly in my face, my womans face.
Whose only beauty is the hate it bears ye;
See with thy narrowest eyes, thy sharpest wishes,
Into my soul, and see what there inhabits;
See if one fear, one shadow of a terror,
One paleness dare appear but from my anger,
To lay hold on your mercies. No, ye fools,
Poor fortunes fools, we were not born for triumphs,
To follow your gay sports, and fill your slaves
With hoots and acclamations.

PETILLIUS
Brave behaviour.

1ST DAUGHTER
The children of as great as Rome, as noble,
Our names before her, and our deeds her envy;
Must we guild ore your Conquest, make your State,
That is not fairly strong, but fortunate?
No, no, ye Romans, we have ways to scape ye,
To make ye poor again, indeed our prisoners,
And stick our triumphs full.

PETILLIUS
's death, I shall love her.

1ST DAUGHTER
To torture ye with suffering, like our slaves;
To make ye curse our patience, wish the world
Were lost again, to win us only, and esteem

The end of all ambitions.

BONDUCA
Do ye wonder?
We'll make our monuments in spite of fortune,
In spight of all your Eagles wings: we'll work
A pitch above ye; and from our height we'll stoop
As fearless of your bloody soars; and fortunate,
As if we prey'd on heartless doves.

SWETONIUS
Strange stiffness.
Decius, go charge the breach.

[Exit **DECIUS**.

BONDUCA
Charge it home, Roman,
We shall deceive thee else. Where's Nennius?

[Enter **NENNIUS**.

NENNIUS
They have made a mighty breach.

BONDUCA
Stick in thy body,
And make it good but half an hour.

NENNIUS
I'll do it.

1ST DAUGHTER
And then be sure to dye.

NENNIUS
It shall go hard else.

BONDUCA
Fare well with all my heart; we shall meet yonder,
Where few of these must come.

NENNIUS
Gods take thee, Lady.

[Exit **NENNIUS**.

BONDUCA

Bring up the swords, and poison.

[Enter **ONE** with Swords, and a great Cup.

2ND DAUGHTER
O my fortune!

BONDUCA
How, how, ye whore?

2ND DAUGHTER
Good mother, nothing to offend ye.

BONDUCA
Here, wench:
Behold us, Romans.

SWETONIUS
Mercy yet.

BONDUCA
No talking:
Puff, there goes all your pitty. Come, short prayers,
And let's dispach the business: you begin,
Shrink not; I'll see ye do't.

2ND DAUGHTER
O gentle mother,
O Romans, O my heart; I dare not.

SWETONIUS
Woman, woman,
Unnatural woman.

2ND DAUGHTER
O perswade her, Romans:
Alass, I am young, and would live. Noble mother,
Can ye kill that ye gave life? are my years
Fit for destruction?

SWETONIUS
Yield, and be a Queen still,
A mother and a friend.

BONDUCA
Ye talk: come, hold it,
And put it home.

1ST DAUGHTER
Fie, sister, fie,
What would you live to be?

BONDUCA
A whore still.

2ND DAUGHTER
Mercy.

SWETONIUS
Hear her, thou wretched woman.

2ND DAUGHTER
Mercy, mother:
O whither will you send me? I was once
Your darling, your delight.

BONDUCA
O gods,
Fear in my family? do it, and nobly.

2ND DAUGHTER
O do not frown then.

1ST DAUGHTER
Do it, worthy Sister:
'Tis nothing, 'tis a pleasure; we'll go with ye.

2ND DAUGHTER
O if I knew but whither.

1ST DAUGHTER
To the blessed,
Where we shall meet our Father.

SWETONIUS
Woman.

BONDUCA
Talk not.

1ST DAUGHTER
Where nothing but true joy is.

BONDUCA
That's a good wench, mine own sweet girl; put it close to thee.

2ND DAUGHTER
Oh comfort me still for heavens sake.

1ST DAUGHTER
Where eternal
Our youths are, and our beauties; where no Wars come,
Nor lustful slaves to ravish us.

2ND DAUGHTER
That steels me:
A long farewel to this world.

BONDUCA
Good: I'll help thee.

1ST DAUGHTER
The next is mine.
Shew me a Roman Lady in all your stories,
Dare do this for her honor: they are cowards,
Eat coals like compell'd Cats: your great Saint Lucrece
Dy'd not for honor; Tarquin topt her well,
And mad she could not hold him, bled.

PETILLIUS
By—
I am in love: I would give an hundred pound now
But to lie with this womans behaviour. Oh the devil.

1ST DAUGHTER
Ye shall see me example, All your Rome,
If I were proud and lov'd ambition;
If I were lustful, all your ways of pleasure;
If I were greedy, all the wealth ye conquer—

BONDUCA
Make haste.

1ST DAUGHTER
I will. Could not intice to live
But two short hours this frailty: would ye learn
How to die bravely Romans, to fling off
This case of flesh, lose all your cares for ever?
Live as we have done, well, and fear the gods,
Hunt Honor, and not Nations with your swords,
Keep your minds humble, your devotions high;
So shall ye learn the noblest part, to die.

[Dies.

BONDUCA

I come, wench; to ye all Fates hangmen; you
That ease the aged destinies, and cut
The threds of Kingdoms, as they draw 'em: here,
Here's the draft would ask no less than Cæsar
To pledge it for the glories sake.

CURIUS

Great Lady.

SWETONIUS

Make up your own conditions.

BONDUCA

So we will.

SWETONIUS

Stay.

DEMETRIUS

Stay.

SWETONIUS

Be any thing.

BONDUCA

A Saint, Swetonius,
When thou shalt fear, and die like a slave. Ye fools,
Ye should have ti'd up death first, when ye conquer'd,
Ye sweat for us in vain else: see him here,
He's ours still, and our friend; laughs at your pities;
And we command him with as easie reins
As do our enemies. I feel the poison.
Poor vanquish'd Romans, with what matchless tortures
Could I now rack ye! But I pittie ye,
Desiring to die quiet: nay, so much
I hate to prosecute my victory,
That I will give ye counsel e'r I die.
If you will keep your Laws and Empire whole,
Place in your Romans flesh, a Britain soul.

[Dies.

[Enter **DECIUS**.

SWETONIUS

Desperate and strange.

DECIUS
'Tis won, Sir, and the Britains
All put to th' sword.

SWETONIUS
Give her fair Funeral;
She was truly noble, and a Queen.

PETILLIUS
—Take it,
A Love-mange grown upon me? what, a spirit?

JUNIUS
I am glad of this, I have found ye.

PETILLIUS
In my belly,
Oh how it tumbles!

JUNIUS
Ye good gods, I thank ye.

[Exeunt.

ACTUS QUINTUS

SCÆNA PRIMA

Enter **CARATACH** upon a rock, and Hengo by him, sleeping.

CARATACH
Thus we afflicted Britains climb for safeties,
And to avoid our dangers, seek destructions;
Thus we awake to sorrows. O thou Woman,
Thou agent for adversities, what curses
This day belong to thy improvidence!
To Britanie by thy means, what sad millions
Of Widows weeping eyes! The strong mans valour
Thou hast betraid to fury; the childs fortune
To fear and want of friends: whose pieties
Might wipe his mournings off, and build his sorrows
A house of rest by his blest Ancestors:
The Virgins thou hast rob'd of all their wishes,
Blasted their blowing hopes, turn'd their songs,
Their mirthful marriage-songs to funerals,

The Land thou hast left a wilderness of wretches.
The boy begins to stir: thy safety made,
Would my soul were in Heaven.

HENGO
O noble Uncle,
Look out: I dream'd we were betrai'd.

[A soft dead march within.

CARATACH
No harm, boy;
'Tis but thy emptiness that breeds these fancies:
Thou shalt have meat anon.

HENGO
A little, Uncle,
And I shall hold out bravely. What are those?
Look, Uncle, look, those multitudes that march there?
They come upon us stealing by.

CARATACH
I see 'em;
And prethee be not fearful.

HENGO
Now ye hate me,
Would I were dead.

CARATACH
Thou know'st I love thee dearly.

HENGO
Did I e'r shrink yet, Uncle? were I a man now;
I should be angry with ye.

[Enter **DRUSIUS**, **REGULUS** and **SOLDIERS** with Penyus's Herse, Drums and Colours.

CARATACH
My sweet chicken,
See, they have reach'd us, and as it seems they bear
Some soldiers body, by their solemn gestures,
And sad solemnities; it well appears too
To be of eminence. Most worthy Soldiers,
Let me intreat your knowledge to inform me
What noble Body that is which you bear
With such a sad and ceremonious grief,
As if ye meant to wooe the World and Nature

To be in love with death? Most honorable
Excellent Romans, by your antient valours,
As ye love Fame, resolve me.

SOLDIER
'Tis the Body
Of the great Captain Penyus, by himself
Made cold and spiritless.

CARATACH
O stay, ye Romans,
By the Religion which you owe those gods
That lead ye on to Victories, by those glories
Which made even pride a virtue in ye.

DRUSIUS
Stay:
What's thy Will, Caratach?

CARATACH
Set down the body,
The body of the noblest of all Romans,
As ye expect an offering at your Graves
From your friends sorrows, set it down awhile.
That with your griefs an enemy may mingle;
A noble enemy that loves a Soldier;
And lend a tear to virtue, even your foes,
Your wild foes, as you call'd us, are yet stor'd
With fair affections, our hearts fresh, our spirits,
Though sometime stubborn, yet when virtue dies,
Soft and relenting as a Virgins prayers,
Oh set it down.

DRUSIUS
Set down the body, soldiers.

CARATACH
Thou hallowed relique, thou rich Diamond
Cut with thine own dust; thou for whose wide fame
The world appears too narrow, mans all thoughts,
Had they all tongues, too silent; thus I bow
To thy most honour'd ashes: though an enemy,
Yet friend to all thy worths: sleep peaceably;
Happiness crown thy soul, and in thy earth
Some Lawrel fix his seat, there grow, and flourish,
And make thy grave an everlasting triumph.
Farewell all glorious Wars, now thou art gone,
And honest Arms adieu: all noble battels

Maintain'd in thirst of honour, not of bloud,
Farewell for ever.

HENGO
Was this Roman, Uncle,
So good a man?

CARATACH
Thou never knew'st thy Father.

HENGO
He dy'd before I was born.

CARATACH
This worthy Roman
Was such another piece of endless honor,
Such a brave soul dwelt in him: their proportions
And faces were not much unlik, boy, excellent nature,
See how it works into his eyes, mine own boy.

HENGO
The multitudes of these men, and their fortunes,
Could never make me fear yet: one mans goodness—

CARATACH
O now thou pleasest me: weep still, my child,
As if thou saw'st me dead; with such a flux
Or flood of sorrow: still thou pleasest me.
And worthy soldiers, pray receive these pledges,
These hatchments of our griefs, and grace us so much
To place 'em on his Hearse. Now if ye please,
Bear off the noble burden; raise his pile
High as Olympus, make heaven to wonder
To see a star upon earth out-shining theirs.
And ever loved, ever living be
Thy honoured and most sacred memory.

DRUSIUS
Thou hast done honestly, good Caratach,
And when thou diest, a thousand virtuous Romans
Shall sing thy soul to heaven. Now march on, soldiers.

[Exeunt. A dead march.

CARATACH
Now dry thine eyes, my boy.

HENGO

Are they all gone?
I could have wept this hour yet.

CARATACH
Come, take cheer,
And raise thy spirit, child: if but this day
Thou canst bear out thy faintness, the night coming
I'll fashion our escape.

HENGO
Pray fear not me;
Indeed I am very hearty.

CARATACH
Be so still;
His mischiefs lessen, that controuls his ill.

[Exeunt.

SCÆNA SECUNDA

Enter **PETILLIUS**.

PETILLIUS
What do I ail, i'th' name of heaven I did but see her,
And see her die: she stinks by this time strongly,
Abominably stinks: she was a woman,
A thing I never car'd for: but to die so,
So confidently, bravely, strongly; Oh the devil,
I have the bots, by—she scorn'd us strangely,
All we could do, or durst do; threatned us
With such a noble anger, and so governed
With such a fiery spirit—; the plain bots;
A—upon the bots, the love-bots: hang me,
Hang me even out o'th' way, directly hang me.
Oh penny pipers, and most painful penners
Of bountiful new Ballads, what a subject,
What a sweet subject for your silver sounds,
Is crept upon ye!

[Enter **JUNIUS**.

JUNIUS
Here he is; have at him.
[**Sings**.
She set the sword unto her Breast,

great pity it was to see,
That three drops of her Life-warm bloud,
run trickling down her knee.
Art thou there, bonny boy? and i'faith how dost thou?

PETILLIUS
Well, gramercie, how dost thou? h'as found me,
Sented me out: the shame the devil ow'd me.
H'as kept his day with. And what news, Junius?

JUNIUS
It was an old tale ten thousand times told,
Of a young Lady was turned into mold,
Her life it was lovely, her death it was bold.

PETILLIUS
A cruel rogue, now h'as drawn pursue on me,
He hunts me like a devil. No more singing;
Thou hast got a cold: come, let's go drink some Sack, boy.

JUNIUS
Ha, ha, ha, ha, ha, ha.

PETILLIUS
Why dost thou laugh?
What Mares nest hast thou found?

JUNIUS
Ha, ha, ha.
I cannot laugh alone: Decius, Demetrius,
Curius, oh my sides, Ha, ha, ha,
The strangest jest.

PETILLIUS
Prethee no more.

JUNIUS
The admirablest fooling.

PETILLIUS
Thou art the prettiest fellow.

JUNIUS
Sirs.

PETILLIUS
Why Junius;
Prethee away, sweet Junius.

JUNIUS
Let me sing then.

PETILLIUS
Whoa, here's a stir now: sing a song o' six pence,
By—if prethee;—on't: Junius.

JUNIUS
I must either sing; or laugh.

PETILLIUS
And what's your reason?

JUNIUS
What's that to you?

PETILLIUS
And I must whistle.

JUNIUS
Do so.
Oh, I hear 'em coming.

PETILLIUS
I have a little business.

JUNIUS
Thou shall not go, believe it: what a Gentleman
Of thy sweet conversation?

PETILLIUS
Captain Junius,
Sweet Captain, let me go with all celerity;
Things are not always one: and do not question,
Nor jeer, nor gybe: none of your doleful Ditties,
Nor your sweet conversation, you will find then
I may be anger'd.

JUNIUS
By no means, Petillius;
Anger a man that never knew passion?
'Tis most impossible: a noble Captain,
A wise and generous Gentleman?

PETILLIUS
Tom Puppie.
Leave this way to abuse me: I have found ye,

But for your mothers sake I will forgive ye.
Your subtil understanding may discover
(As you think) some trim toy to make you merry;
Some straw to tickle ye; but do not trust to't;
Y' are a young man, and may do well: be sober:
Carry your self discreetly.

[Enter **DECIUS, DEMETRIUS, CURIUS.**

JUNIUS
Yes forsooth.

DEMETRIUS
How does the brave Petillius?

JUNIUS
Monstrous merry:
We two were talking what a kind of thing
I was when I was in love; what a strange monster
For little Boys and Girls to wonder at;
How like a fool I lookt.

DECIUS
So they do all,
Like great dull slavering fools.

JUNIUS
Petillius saw too.

PETILLIUS
No more of this, 'tis scurvie, peace.

JUNIUS
How nastily,
Indeed, how beastly all I did became me!
How I forgot to blow my nose! there he stands,
An honest and a wise man; if himself
(I dare avouch it boldly, for I know it)
Should find himself in love—

PETILLIUS
I am angry.

JUNIUS
Surely his wise self would hang his beastly self,
His understanding-self so mawl his ass-self—

DECIUS

He's bound to do it; for he knows the follies,
The poverties, and baseness that belongs to't,
H'as read upon the reformations long.

PETILLIUS
He has so.

JUNIUS
'Tis true, and he must do't:
Nor is it fit indeed any such coward—

PETILLIUS
You'll leave prating.

JUNIUS
Should dare come near the Regiments, especially
Those curious puppies (for believe there are such)
That only love behaviours: those are dog-whelps,
Dwindle away, because a Woman dies well;
Commit with passions only: fornicate
With the free spirit merely: you, Petillius,
For you have long observ'd the World.

PETILLIUS
Dost thou hear?
I'll beat thee damnably within these three hours:
Go pray; may be I'll kill thee. Farewel Jack-daws.

[Exit.

DECIUS
What a strange thing he's grown!

JUNIUS
I am glad he is so;
And stranger he shall be before I leave him.

CURIUS
Is't possible her mere death—

JUNIUS
I observ'd him,
And found him taken, infinitely taken
With her bravery, I have follow'd him,
And seen him kiss his sword since, court his scabbard,
Call dying, dainty deer; her brave mind, Mistriss;
Casting a thousand ways, to give those forms,
That he might lie with 'em, and get old Armors:

He had got me o' th' hip once: it shall go hard, friends,
But he shall find his own coin.

[Enter **MACER**.

DECIUS
How now Macer?
Is Judas yet come in?

[Enter **JUDAS**.

MACER
Yes, and has lost
Most of his men too. Here he is.

CARATACH
What news?

JUDAS
I have lodg'd him; rouze him he that dares.

DEMETRIUS
Where, Judas?

JUDAS
On a steep rock i'th' woods, the boy too with him,
And there he swears he will keep his Christmas Gentlemen,
But he will come away with full conditions,
Bravely, and like a Britain: he paid part of us.
Yet I think we fought bravely: for mine own part,
I was four several times at half sword with him,
Twice stood his partizan: but the plain truth is,
He's a meer devil, and no man; i'th' end he swing'd us,
And swing'd us soundly too, he fights by Witchcraft:
Yet for all that I see him lodg'd.

JUNIUS
Take more men,
And scout him round. Macer, march you along.
What victuals has he?

JUDAS
Not a piece of Bisket,
Not so much as will stop a tooth; nor Water,
More than they make themselves: they lie
Just like a brace of Bear-whelps, close, and crafty,
Sucking their fingers for their food.

DECIUS
Cut off then
All hope of that way: take sufficient forces.

JUNIUS
But use no foul play, on your lives: that man
That does him mischief by deceit, I'll kill him.

MACER
He shall have fair play, he deserves it.

JUDAS
Hark ye.
What should I do there then? you are brave Captains,
Most valiant men; go up your selves; use virtue,
See what will come on't: pray the Gentleman
To come down, and be taken. Ye all know him,
I think ye have felt him too: there ye shall find him,
His sword by his side, plums of a pound weight by him
Will make your chops ake: you'll find it a more labour
To win him living, than climbing of a Crows-nest.

DECIUS
Away, and compass him; we shall come up
I am sure within these two hours. Watch him close.

MACER
He shall flee thorow the air, if he escape us.

[A sad noise within.

JUNIUS
What's this loud lamentation?

MACER
The dead body
Of the great Penyus is new come to the Camp, Sir.

DEMETRIUS
Dead!

MACER
By himself, they say.

JUNIUS
I fear'd that fortune.

CURIUS

Peace guide him up to heaven.

JUNIUS
Away good Macer.

[Exeunt **MACER** and **JUDAS**.

[Enter **SWETONIUS, DRUSIUS, REGULUS, PETILLIUS**.

SWETONIUS
If thou be'st guilty,
Some sullen plague thou hat'st most light upon thee:
The Regiment return on Junius,
He well deserves it.

PETILLIUS
So.

SWETONIUS
Draw out three Companies,
Yours Decius, Junius, and thou Petillius,
And make up instantly to Caratach,
He's in the Wood before ye; we shall follow
After due ceremony done to the dead,
The noble dead: Come: let's go burn the Body.

[Exeunt all but **PETILLIUS**.

PETILLIUS
The Regiment given from me; disgrac'd openly;
In love too with a trifle to abuse me?
A merry world, a fine world: serv'd seven years
To be an ass o' both sides, sweet Petillius,
You have brought your hogs to a fine market; you are wise, Sir,
Your honourable brain-pan full of crotchets,
An understanding Gentleman; your projects
Cast with assurance ever: wouldst not thou now
Be bang'd about the pate, Petillius
Answer to that sweet soldier; surely, surely,
I think ye would; pull'd by the nose, kick'd; hang thee,
Thou art the arrant'st Rascal: trust thy wisdom
With any thing of weight; the wind with feathers.
Out ye blind puppie; you command? you govern?
Dig for a groat a day, or serve a Swine-herd;
Too noble for thy nature too. I must up;
But what I shall do there, let time discover.

[Exit.

SCÆNIA TERTIA

Enter **MACER** and **JUDAS**, with meat and a bottle.

MACER
Hang it o'th' side o'th' rock, as though the Britains
Stole hither to relieve him; who first ventures
To fetch it off, is ours. I cannot see him.

JUDAS
He lies close in a hole above, I know it,
Gnawing upon his anger: ha? no, 'tis not he.

MACER
'Tis but the shaking of the boughs.

JUDAS
—Shake 'em,
I am sure they shake me soundly. There.

MACER
'Tis nothing.

JUDAS
Make no noise if he stir, a deadly tempest
Of huge stones fall upon us: 'tis done: away close.

[Exit.

[Enter **CARATACH**.

CARATACH
Sleep still, sleep sweetly child, 'tis all thou feedst on.
No gentle Britain near; no valiant charity
To bring thee food? poor knave, thou art sick extreme sick,
Almost grown wild for meat; and yet thy goodness
Will not confess, nor shew it. All the woods
Are double lin'd with soldiers; no way left us
To make a noble scape: I'll sit down by thee,
And when thou wak'st, either get meat to save thee,
Or lose my life i'th' purchase, Good gods comfort thee.

[Enter **JUNIUS, DECIUS, PETILLIUS, GUIDE**.

GUIDE

Ye are not far off now, Sir.

JUNIUS
Draw the Companies
The closest way thorow the woods; we'll keep on this way.

GUIDE
I will Sir: half a furlong more you'll come
Within the sight o'th' Rock; keep on the left side,
You'll be discover'd else: I'll lodge your Companies
In the wild Vines beyond ye.

DECIUS
Do ye mark him?

JUNIUS
Yes, and am sorry for him.

PETILLIUS
Junius,
Pray let me speak two words with you.

JUNIUS
Walk afore,
I'll overtake ye straight.

DECIUS
I will.

[Exit.

JUNIUS
Now, Captain.

PETILLIUS
You have oft told me, you have lov'd me, Junius.

JUNIUS
Most sure I told you truth then.

PETILLIUS
And that love
Should not deny me any honest thing.

JUNIUS
It shall not.

PETILLIUS

Dare ye swear it?
I have forgot all passages between us
That have been ill, forgiven too, forgot you.

JUNIUS
What would this man have? By—I do, Sir,
So it be fit to grant ye.

PETILLIUS
'Tis most honest.

JUNIUS
Why, then I'll do it.

PETILLIUS
Kill me.

JUNIUS
How?

PETILLIUS
Pray kill me.

JUNIUS
Kill ye?

PETILLIUS
I, kill me quickly, suddenly,
Now kill me.

JUNIUS
On what reason? ye amaze me.

PETILLIUS
If ye do love me, kill me, ask me not why:
I would be killed, and by you.

JUNIUS
Mercy on me,
What ails this man? Petillius.

PETILLIUS
Pray ye dispatch me,
Ye are not safe whilst I live: I am dangerous,
Troubled extreamly, even to mischief, Junius,
An enemy to all good men: fear not, 'tis justice;
I shall kill you else.

JUNIUS

Tell me but the cause,
And I will do it.

PETILLIUS

I am disgrac'd, my service
Slighted, and unrewarded by the General,
My hopes left wild and naked; besides these,
I am grown ridiculous, an ass, a folly
I dare not trust my self with: prethee kill me.

JUNIUS

All these may be redeem'd as easily
As you would heal your finger.

PETILLIUS

Nay—

JUNIUS

Stay, I'll do it,
You shall not need your anger: But first, Petillius,
You shall unarm your self; I dare not trust
A man so bent to mischief.

PETILLIUS

There's my sword;
And do it handsomely.

JUNIUS

Yes, I will kill ye,
Believe that certain: but first I'll lay before ye
The most extreme fool ye have plaid in this,
The honor purpos'd for ye, the great honor
The General intended ye.

PETILLIUS

How?

JUNIUS

And then I'll kill ye,
Because ye shall die miserable. Know Sir,
The Regiment was given me, but till time
Call'd ye to do some worthy deed, might stop
The peoples ill thoughts of ye, for Lord Penyus,
I mean his death. How soon this time's come to ye,
And hasted by Swetonius? Go, says he,
Junius and Decius, and go thou Petillius;
Distinctly, thou Petillius, and draw up,

To take stout Caratach; there's the deed purpos'd,
A deed to take off all faults, of all natures:
And thou Petillius; Mark it, there's the honor,
And that done, all made even.

PETILLIUS
Stay.

JUNIUS
No, I'll kill ye.
He knew thee absolute, and full in soldier,
Daring beyond all dangers, found thee out
According to the boldness of thy spirit,
A Subject, such a Subject.

PETILLIUS
Harke ye Junius,
I will live now.

JUNIUS
By no means. Wooed thy worth,
Held thee by the chin up, as thou sunk'st, and shew'd thee
How Honor held her arms out: Come, make ready,
Since ye will die an ass.

PETILLIUS
Thou wilt not kill me?

JUNIUS
By—but I will, Sir: I'll have no man dangerous
Live to destroy me afterward. Besides, you have gotten
Honor enough, let young men rise now. Nay,
I do perceive too by the General, (which is
One main cause ye shall die) howe'r he carry it,
Such a strong doting on ye, that I fear,
You shall command in chief: how are we paid then?
Come, if you will pray, dispatch it.

PETILLIUS
Is there no way?

JUNIUS
Not any way to live.

PETILLIUS
I will do any thing,
Redeem my self at any price: good Junius,
Let me but die upon the Rock, but offer

My life up like a Soldier.

JUNIUS
You will seek then
To out-doe every man.

PETILLIUS
Believe it Junius,
You shall goe stroke by stroke with me.

JUNIUS
You'll leave off too,
As you are noble, and a soldier,
For ever these mad fancies.

PETILLIUS
Dare ye trust me?
By all that's good and honest.

JUNIUS
There's your sword then,
And now come on a new man: Virtue guide thee.

[Exeunt.

[Enter **CARATACH** and **HENGO** on the Rock.

CARATACH
Courage my Boy, I have found meat: look Hengo,
Look where some blessed Britain, to preserve thee,
Has hung a little food and drink: cheer up Boy,
Do not forsake me now.

HENGO
O Uncle. Uncle,
I feel I cannot stay long: yet I'll fetch it,
To keep your noble life: Uncle, I am heart-whole,
And would live.

CARATACH
Thou shalt, long I hope.

HENGO
But my head, Uncle:
Methinks the Rock goes round.

[Enter **MACER** and **JUDAS**.

MACER
Mark 'em well, Judas.

JUDAS
Peace, as you love your life.

HENGO
Do not you hear
The noise of Bels?

CARATACH
Of Bels Boy? 'tis thy fancie,
Alas, thy bodies full of wind.

HENGO
Methinks, Sir,
They ring a strange sad knell, a preparation
To some near funeral of State: nay, weep not,
Mine own sweet Uncle, you will kill me sooner.

CARATACH
Oh my poor chicken.

HENGO
Fie, faint-hearted Uncle:
Come, tie me in your Belt, and let me down.

CARATACH
I'll go my self Boy.

HENGO
No, as ye love me, Uncle;
I will not eat it, if I do not fetch it;
The danger only I desire: pray tie me.

CARATACH
I will, and all my care hang o'r thee: come child,
My valiant child.

HENGO
Let me down apace, Uncle,
And ye shall see how like a Daw I'll whip it
From all their policies: for 'tis most certain
A Roman train: and ye must hold me sure too,
You'll spoil all else. When I have brought it Uncle,
We'll be as merry—

CARATACH

Go i'th' name of heaven, Boy.

HENGO
Quick, quick, Uncle, I have it. Oh.

[**JUDAS** shoots **HENGO**.

CARATACH
What ail'st thou?

HENGO
O my best Uncle, I am slain.

CARATACH
I see ye, and heaven direct my hand: destruction

[**CARATACH** kills **JUDAS** with a stone from the rock.

Go with thy coward soul. How dost thou Boy?
Oh villain, pocky villain.

HENGO
Oh Uncle, Uncle,
Oh how it pricks me: am I preserv'd for this?
Extremely pricks me.

CARATACH
Coward, rascal Coward,
Dogs eat thy flesh.

HENGO
Oh I bleed hard: I faint too, out upon't,
How sick I am! the lean Rogue, Uncle.

CARATACH
Look Boy,
I have laid him sure enough.

HENGO
Have ye knockt his brains out?

CARATACH
I warrant thee for stirring more: cheer up, child.

HENGO
Hold my sides hard, stop, stop, oh wretched fortune,
Must we part thus? Still I grow sicker, Uncle.

CARATACH

Heaven look upon this noble child.

HENGO

I once hop'd
I should have liv'd to have met these bloody Romans
At my swords point, to have reveng'd my Father,
To have beaten 'em: oh hold me hard. But Uncle—

CARATACH

Thou shalt live still I hope Boy. Shall I draw it?

HENGO

Ye draw away my soul then, I would live
A little longer; spare me heavens, but only
To thank you for your tender love. Good Uncle,
Good noble Uncle weep not.

CARATACH

Oh my chicken,
My dear Boy, what shall I lose?

HENGO

Why, a child,
That must have died however: had this scap'd me,
Feaver or famine—I was born to die, Sir.

CARATACH

But thus unblown, my boy?

HENGO

I go the straighter
My journey to the gods: Sure I shall know ye
When ye come, Uncle.

CARATACH

Yes, Boy.

HENGO

And I hope
We shall enjoy together that great blessedness
You told me of.

CARATACH

Most certain, child.

HENGO

I grow cold,

Mine eyes are going.

CARATACH
Lift 'em up.

HENGO
Pray for me;
And noble Uncle, when my bones are ashes,
Think of your little Nephew. Mercy.

CARATACH
Mercy.
You blessed Angels take him.

HENGO
Kiss me: so.
Farewel, farewel.

[Dies.

CARATACH
Farewel the hopes of Britain,
Thou Royal graft, Farewel for ever. Time and Death,
Ye have done your worst. Fortune now see, now proudly
Pluck off thy vail, and view thy triumph: Look
Look what thou hast brought this Land to. Oh fair flower,
How lovely yet thy ruines show, how sweetly
Even death embraces thee! The peace of heaven,
The fellowship of all great souls be with thee.

[Enter **PETILLIUS** and **JUNIUS** on the rock.

Hah? dare ye Romans? ye shall win me bravely.
Thou art mine.

[Fight.

JUNIUS
Not yet, Sir.

CARATACH
Breath ye, ye poor Romans,
And come up all, with all your antient valors,
Like a rough wind I'll shake your souls, and send 'em—

[Enter **SWETONIUS** and all the Roman **CAPTAINS**.

SWETONIUS

Yield thee bold Caratach; by all—
As I am Soldier, as I envie thee,
I'll use thee like thy self, the valiant Britain.

PETILLIUS
Brave soldier yield; thou stock of Arms and Honor,
Thou filler of the World with Fame and Glory.

JUNIUS
Most worthy man, we'll wooe thee, be thy prisoners.

SWETONIUS
Excellent Britain, do me but that Honor,
That more to me than Conquests, that true happiness,
To be my friend.

CARATACH
Oh Romans, see what here is:
Had this Boy liv'd—

SWETONIUS
For Fames sake, for thy Swords sake,
As thou desirest to build thy virtues greater:
By all that's excellent in man, and honest—

CARATACH
I do believe: Ye have had me a brave foe;
Make me a noble friend, and from your goodness,
Give this Boy honourable earth to lie in.

SWETONIUS
He shall have fitting Funeral.

CARATACH
I yield then.
Not to your blows, but your brave courtesies.

PETILLIUS
Thus we conduct then to the arms of Peace
The wonder of the World.

SWETONIUS
Thus I embrace thee,

[Flourish.

And let it be no flattery that I tell thee,
Thou art the only Soldier.

CARATACH
How to thank ye,
I must hereafter find upon your usage.
I am for Rome.

SWETONIUS
Ye must.

CARATACH
Then Rome shall know
The man that makes her spring of glory grow.

SWETONIUS
Petillius, you have shown much worth this day,
redeem'd much error,
Ye have my love again, preserve it, Junius,
With you I make him equal in the Regiment.

JUNIUS
The elder and the nobler: I'll give place, Sir.

SWETONIUS
Ye shew a friends soul.

March on, and through the Camp in every tongue,
The Virtues of great Caratach be sung.

[Exeunt.

John Fletcher – A Short Biography

John Fletcher was born in December, 1579 in Rye, Sussex. He was baptised on December 20th.

As can be imagined details of much of his life and career have not survived and, accordingly, only a very brief indication of his life and works can be given.

His father, Richard Fletcher, was a successful and rather ambitious cleric. From being the Dean of Peterborough he moved on to become the Bishop of Bristol, Bishop of Worcester and finally, shortly before his death, the Bishop of London. He was also the chaplain to Queen Elizabeth.

When he was Dean of Peterborough, Richard Fletcher, witnessed the execution of Mary, Queen of Scots. It was said he "knelt down on the scaffold steps and started to pray out loud and at length, in a prolonged and rhetorical style, as though determined to force his way into the pages of history". He cried out at her death, "So perish all the Queen's enemies!" All very dramatic but the family did have strong links to the Arts.

Young Fletcher appears at the very young age of eleven to have entered Corpus Christi College at Cambridge University in 1591. There are no records that he ever took a degree but there is some small evidence that he was being prepared for a career in the church.

However what is clear is that this was soon abandoned as he joined the stream of people who would leave University and decamp to the more bohemian life of commercial theatre in London.

Unfortunately his father fell out with Queen Elizabeth but appears to have been on his way to rehabilitation before his death in 1596. At his death he was, however, mired in debt.

The upbringing of the now teenage Fletcher and his seven siblings now passed to his paternal uncle, the poet and minor official Giles Fletcher. Giles, who had the patronage of the Earl of Essex may have been a liability rather than an advantage to the young Fletcher. With Essex involved in the failed rebellion against Elizabeth Giles was also tainted by association.

By 1606 John Fletcher appears to have equipped himself with the talents to become a playwright. Initially this appears to have been for the Children of the Queen's Revels, then performing at the Blackfriars Theatre.

Commendatory verses by Richard Brome in the Beaumont and Fletcher 1647 folio place Fletcher in the company of Ben Jonson, although it is not known when this friendship began. Jonson, of course, was a leviathan of English Literature, so admired that many of his literary friends and colleagues were simply known as 'Sons of Ben'. Fletcher's frequent early collaborator, Francis Beaumont, was also a friend of Jonson's.

Fletcher's early career was marked by one significant failure; The Faithful Shepherdess, his adaptation of Giovanni Battista Guarini's Il Pastor Fido, which was performed by the Blackfriars Children in 1608. In the preface to the printed edition of his play, Fletcher explained the failure as due to his audience's faulty expectations. They expected a pastoral tragicomedy to feature dances, comedy, and murder, with the shepherds presented in conventional stereotypes – as Fletcher put it, wearing "gray cloaks, with curtailed dogs in strings." Fletcher's preface is however best known for its pithy definition of tragicomedy: "A tragicomedy is not so called in respect of mirth and killing, but in respect it wants [i.e., lacks] deaths, which is enough to make it no tragedy; yet brings some near it, which is enough to make it no comedy." A comedy, he went on to say, must be "a representation of familiar people." His preface is critical of drama that features characters whose action violates nature.

In that case, Fletcher appears to have been developing a new style faster than audiences could comprehend. By 1609, however, he had found his stride. With Beaumont, he wrote Philaster, which became a hit for the King's Men and began a profitable association between Fletcher and that company. Philaster appears also to have begun a trend for tragicomedy. Fletcher's influence has also been said to have inspired some features of Shakespeare's late romances, and certainly his influence on the tragicomic work of other playwrights is even more marked.

By the middle of the 1610s, Fletcher's plays had achieved a popularity that rivalled Shakespeare's and cemented the pre-eminence of the King's Men in Jacobean London. After Beaumont's retirement, necessitated by ill-health, and then his early death in 1616, Fletcher continued working, both singly and in collaboration, until his death in 1625. By that time, he had produced, or had been credited with, close to fifty plays. This body of work remained a major part of the King's Men's repertory until the closing of the theatres in 1642 due to the Civil War.

At the beginning of his career Fletcher's most important collaborator was Francis Beaumont. The two wrote together for close to a decade, first for the Children of the Queen's Revels, and then for the King's Men. According to an anecdote transmitted or invented by John Aubrey, they also lived together in Bankside, sharing clothes and having "one wench in the house between them." This domestic arrangement, if it existed, was ended by Beaumont's marriage in 1613, and their dramatic partnership ended after Beaumont fell ill, probably of a stroke, that same year.

At this point Fletcher had written many plays with Beaumont and several others on his own. He seems to have been regarded as quite a talent although it should be remembered that playwrights were required to be prolific, to easily work with other collaborators and to produce work of quality and commercial appeal very quickly.

The King's Men, run by Philip Henslowe, was the most prestigious of the theatre companies and Fletcher now had an increasingly close association with it.

Fletcher collaborated with Shakespeare on Henry VIII, The Two Noble Kinsmen, and the now lost Cardenio, which some scholars say was the basis for Lewis Theobald's play Double Falsehood. (Theobald is regarded as one of the best Shakespearean editors. Whether his play is based on Cardenio or on some other is not absolutely known although Theobald certainly promoted it as his revision of the lost Shakespeare/Fletcher play.)

A play that Fletcher also wrote by himself at this time, The Woman's Prize or the Tamer Tamed, is also regarded as a sequel to The Taming of the Shrew.

In 1616, with the death of Shakespeare, Fletcher now appears to have entered into an enhanced arrangement with the King's Men on very similar terms to Shakespeare's. Fletcher would now write exclusively for the King's Men until his own death almost a decade later.

As well as continuing his solo productions Fletcher was still collaborating with other playwrights, mainly Philip Massinger, who, in turn, would succeed him as the in-house playwright for the King's Men.

Fletcher's popularity continued throughout his life; indeed during the winter of 1621, he had three of his plays performed at court. His mastery is most notable in two dramatic types; tragicomedy and the comedy of manners.

John Fletcher died in 1625, it is thought of bubonic plague which, at the time, was undergoing further outbreaks.

He seems to have been buried in what is now Southwark Cathedral, although a precise location is not known. There is much made of an anecdote that Fletcher and Massinger (who died in 1640) share the same grave but it is more likely that both are buried within a few yards of each other and that the stone markers in the floor have confused the issue. One is marked 'Edmond Shakespeare 1607' and the other 'John Fletcher 1625' refers to Shakespeare's younger brother and the playwright. The churchyards were, more often than not, completely over-crowded and breeding grounds for disease. Precise record keeping was not a practiced skill.

During the later Commonwealth, many of the playwright's best-known scenes were kept alive as drolls. These were brief performances, usually condensed into one or two scenes and with the addition of music or song to satisfy the taste for plays while the theatres were closed under the Puritans. At the re-opening of the theatres in 1660, the plays in the Fletcher canon, in original form or revised, were by far the most common productions on the English stage. The most frequently revived plays suggest the developing taste for comedies of manners. Among the tragedies, The Maid's Tragedy and, especially, Rollo Duke of Normandy held the stage. Four tragicomedies (A King and No King, The Humorous Lieutenant, Philaster, and The Island Princess) were popular, perhaps in part for their similarity to and foreshadowing of heroic drama. Four comedies (Rule a Wife And Have a Wife, The Chances, Beggars' Bush, and especially The Scornful Lady) were also stage mainstays.

Despite his popularity, and it appears he was held in higher regard than Shakespeare at this time, his works steadily lost ground to those of Shakespeare and to new productions from other playwrights.

Since then Fletcher has increasingly become a subject only for occasional revivals and for specialists. Fletcher and his collaborators have been the subject of important bibliographic and critical studies, but the plays have been revived only infrequently.

Due to the frequent collaborations between all manner of playwrights, and the revisions carried out in later years, having a settled list of authorship to any given set of plays can be problematic. The works of Fletcher and others of this period most definitely fall into this category. It is as well to take into account that during this period theatres were quite often closed either due to outbreaks of the plague or to the prevailing political and moral climate. Printers, anxious to provide materials that would sell, were not above changing a name or two to enhance sales.

Although Fletcher collaborated most often with Beaumont and Massinger, it is believed that Massinger revised many of the plays some time after their original production. Other collaborators including Nathan Field, William Shakespeare, William Rowley and others also can be seen distinctly in Fletchers' works. Many modern scholars point out that Fletcher had many particular mannerisms but other playwrights would also duplicate these at times so allocating exact contributions of anyone to a play is somewhat of a detective case in many instances. However from the original folio printings or licensing via the Master of the Revels (the statutory licensing authority to approve and censor plays as well a hand in publication and printing of theatrical materials) as well as contemporary notes a fairly precise bibliography of the works can be given with only a few plays lacking substantial authority and provenance.

This bibliography gives the most likely date of writing together with when published, revised or licensed by the Master or the Revels (This position within the royal household was originally for royal festivities, ie revels, and later to oversee stage censorship, until this function was transferred to the Lord Chamberlain in 1624).

Solo Plays
The Faithful Shepherdess, pastoral (written 1608–9; printed 1609)

The Tragedy of Valentinian, tragedy (1610–14; 1647)
Monsieur Thomas, comedy (c. 1610–16; 1639)
The Woman's Prize, or The Tamer Tamed, comedy (c. 1611; 1647)
Bonduca, tragedy (1611–14; 1647)
The Chances, comedy (c. 1613–25; 1647)
Wit Without Money, comedy (c. 1614; 1639)
The Mad Lover, tragicomedy (acted 5 January 1617; 1647)
The Loyal Subject, tragicomedy (licensed 16 November 1618; revised 1633; 1647)
The Humorous Lieutenant, tragicomedy (c. 1619; 1647)
Women Pleased, tragicomedy (c. 1619–23; 1647)
The Island Princess, tragicomedy (c. 1620; 1647)
The Wild Goose Chase, comedy (c. 1621; 1652)
The Pilgrim, comedy (c. 1621; 1647)
A Wife for a Month, tragicomedy (licensed 27 May 1624; 1647)
Rule a Wife and Have a Wife, comedy (licensed 19 October 1624; 1640)

Collaborations

With Francis Beaumont
The Woman Hater, comedy (1606; 1607)
Cupid's Revenge, tragedy (c. 1607–12; 1615)
Philaster, or Love Lies a-Bleeding, tragicomedy (c. 1609; 1620)
The Maid's Tragedy, Tragedy (c. 1609; 1619)
A King and No King, tragicomedy (1611; 1619)
The Captain, comedy (c. 1609–12; 1647)
The Scornful Lady, comedy (c. 1613; 1616)
Love's Pilgrimage, tragicomedy (c. 1615–16; 1647)
The Noble Gentleman, comedy (c. 1613; licensed 3 February 1626; 1647)

With Francis Beaumont & Philip Massinger
Thierry & Theodoret, tragedy (c. 1607; 1621)
The Coxcomb, comedy (c. 1608–10; 1647)
Beggars' Bush, comedy (c. 1612–13; revised 1622; 1647)
Love's Cure, comedy (c. 1612–13; revised 1625; 1647)

With Philip Massinger
Sir John van Olden Barnavelt, tragedy (August 1619; MS)
The Little French Lawyer, comedy (c. 1619–23; 1647)
A Very Woman, tragicomedy (c. 1619–22; licensed 6 June 1634; 1655)
The Custom of the Country, comedy (c. 1619–23; 1647)
The Double Marriage, tragedy (c. 1619–23; 1647)
The False One, history (c. 1619–23; 1647)
The Prophetess, tragicomedy (licensed 14 May 1622; 1647)
The Sea Voyage, comedy (licensed 22 June 1622; 1647)
The Spanish Curate, comedy (licensed 24 October 1622; 1647)
The Lovers' Progress or The Wandering Lovers, tragicomedy (licensed 6 December 1623; rev 1634; 1647)
The Elder Brother, comedy (c. 1625; 1637)

The Honest Man's Fortune, tragicomedy (1613; 1647)
The Queen of Corinth, tragicomedy (c. 1616–18; 1647)
The Knight of Malta, tragicomedy (c. 1619; 1647)

With William Shakespeare
Henry VIII, history (c. 1613; 1623)
The Two Noble Kinsmen, tragicomedy (c. 1613; 1634)
Cardenio, tragicomedy (c. 1613)

With Thomas Middleton & William Rowley
Wit at Several Weapons, comedy (c. 1610–20; 1647)

With William Rowley
The Maid in the Mill (licensed 29 August 1623; 1647).

With Nathan Field
Four Plays, or Moral Representations, in One, morality (c. 1608–13; 1647)

With Philip Massinger, Ben Jonson and George Chapman
Rollo Duke of Normandy, or The Bloody Brother, tragedy (c. 1617; revised 1627–30; 1639)

With James Shirley
The Night Walker, or The Little Thief, comedy (c. 1611; 1640)
The Coronation c. 1635

Uncertain
The Nice Valour, or The Passionate Madman, comedy (c. 1615–25; 1647)
The Laws of Candy, tragicomedy (c. 1619–23; 1647)
The Fair Maid of the Inn, comedy (licensed 22 January 1626; 1647)
The Faithful Friends, tragicomedy (registered 29 June 1660; MS.)

The Nice Valour is possibly by Fletcher revised by Thomas Middleton;

The Fair Maid of the Inn is perhaps a play by Massinger, John Ford, and John Webster, either with or without Fletcher's involvement.

The Laws of Candy has been variously attributed to Fletcher and to John Ford.

The Night-Walker was a Fletcher original, with additions by Shirley for a 1639 production.

Even now there is not absolute certainty on several of the plays. The first Beaumont & Fletcher folio of 1647 contained 35 plays and the second folio of 1679 added a further 18. In total 53 plays.

The first folio included The Masque of the Inner Temple and Gray's Inn (1613), and the second The Knight of the Burning Pestle (1607), widely considered Beaumont's solo works, although the latter was in early editions attributed to both writers. Fletcher himself said that Beaumont was attributed so-authorship of many works that belonged solely to Fletcher or to other collaborators.

One play in the canon, Sir John Van Olden Barnavelt, existed in manuscript and was not published till 1883.

www.ingramcontent.com/pod-product-compliance
Lightning Source LLC
Chambersburg PA
CBHW060114050426
42448CB00010B/1859